A MAVERICK MUSINGS

ASHOKAN SRINIVASAN

BlueRose
Publishers

First Published in December 2020

ISBN: 978-93-5427-129-8

-

BLUEROSE PUBLISHERS

www.bluerosepublishers.com

info@bluerosepublishers.com

+91 8882 898 898

Cover Design:

Mohd. Arif

Typographic Design:

Namrata Saini

Distributed by: BlueRose, Amazon, Flipkart, Shopclues

To my darling angels

Alekhya

Abhinaya

ACKNOWLEDGEMENTS

As they say, it takes a village - and I owe my gratitude to some wonderful people who directly or indirectly helped. First, I would like to thank my friend V. Mathivanan, who has been by my side for most of my life. More than a friend, he has been a guide to me; it was he who ushered me into the world of Objectivism and introduced me to the writings of Ayn Rand. He has been a tutor who inculcated in me the philosophy of *Vishishta-Advaitham*. Not the one to ever say no, he has also been my travel companion on the road trips to various temples across India.

My cousin, Raja Sundaram, who lives in Malaysia, has always stood with me in my times of distress and has been the first one to show me how travel helps to recuperate from an emotional scar. It was he who organised most of my South East Asia trips.

My brother-in-law from Singapore, Gnasegaran Yacob, a travel enthusiast who has travelled to more than a hundred countries and always has his rucksack ready to explore more. He taught me the art of thrifty travelling and I feel proud to have travelled with him on two thrilling road trips.

My friend, Vinod Morsa, settled in Seattle, USA, has always been there for me when I needed any logistical support during my travels. He had planned a few trips for me and if I can brag about staying at the Hiltons the world over, it was due to his sponsorship. His kindness knows no bounds. There were times when I ran out of money in my travels and he would immediately replenish my account without me even asking for it.

My teacher, Rishikesh Chhabra, taught me to swing my legs gracefully to Latin music and opened up a path to happiness through dancing. If not for him, my South American trip would have been a damp squib. Not just that, his valuable suggestions and contributions in shaping up this book are also highly appreciated.

My boss, M.B. Manoharan, had all the confidence in me, and in my writings. Had it not been for him, this book wouldn't have seen the light of day.

My friends Sivakumar, Venkat, Ajit Yadav and Syed Hassan have helped in providing feedback to my numerous drafts and, at times, were merciless when it came to criticising. Their feedback has helped in presenting my work in a better way.

Finally I thank my parents, Shanti and S.S. Vasan, who brought me to this beautiful world, and without whom I wouldn't be who I am today.

ASHOKAN SRINIVASAN

PREFACE

At last, I penned it! All the travel encounters and the ruminations my mind played host to are now in print. Travel was a fantasy for me as a child. It later turned into a passion and now is a full-blown addiction. Growing up, I was too shy, and as expected, I always preferred being a backbencher at school. Scared of any attention in the class, the last thing I wished for was being addressed by the teacher. The glare and focus of the whole class made me so nervous that I wanted the ground to open up and gulp me at once. Fast forward to my college days, I came out of the cocoon to wholeheartedly embrace people around me and experience the beauty of this world.

Travelling played a significant role in this transformation. Each journey was an adventure - sometimes challenging and daunting on numerous other occasions. Today if I boast of being an outgoing individual, the credit indeed goes to my travels that provided exposure to various cultures, mindsets, and frequently out-of-the-world conversations. Every journey I undertook, I made it a point to write down a journal of events that have now helped me arrange and meaningfully present my experiences and emotions.

This book unveils my feelings, passions, and sentiments by looking back at the essence of my travels spread over twenty years. The various episodes that occurred and the characters from all those trips mentioned in the book are genuine. I hope this book would give you, the reader, the pleasure of walking with me on my travels and also help you appreciate how it transformed me into a better version of myself. If even one person relates to my experiences and hence takes up to travelling as a passion after reading the book, I would consider myself a good author.

As the indomitable Simon Raven noted insightfully –

"Since life is short, and the world is wide, the sooner you start exploring it, the better."

ASHOKAN SRINIVASAN

Miami International Airport was bustling with commuters. People were swarming the departure counters like a hive of busy ants. It was 6 PM. I had just landed from Bogota and I had to check-in at the Turkish Airlines counter for my onward journey to Chennai via Istanbul and New Delhi. My eyes were weary and I would have given the world in exchange for a couple of hours of comfortable sleep. With that luxury not in the offing, I went to locate my departure counter and stood in the long line, waiting for my turn to check-in. The serpentine line was moving at a snail's pace as there were only a few counters open to handle the passengers. The flight to Istanbul would be 14 hours long and then the connection to New Delhi another 6 hours, not to speak of a 3 hour flight from New Delhi to Chennai. My journey would be horrible if I were allotted a window or a middle seat with little space to stretch. Keeping my worries at bay and pushing my cart inch by inch, I got to one of the counters in another 30 minutes.

There was this pretty lady at the counter who welcomed me with a smile and took my passport. Looking at my itinerary, she said, "Wow! That's one hell of a journey!" I said, "Yeah if you add my flight from Bogota to Miami to this itinerary, it would sure be one hell of an arduous journey!" Seeing an opportunity, I chipped in immediately. "Lady, would you mind putting me in an emergency exit seat so that I can get some leg room?" She looked at me for a second, tore the boarding pass she had just printed, and left. After a few minutes, she came back and gave me my new boarding passes. Yes! To my utter delight, she allotted me a seat near the emergency exit for the journey up to New Delhi. I was surprised! I asked her, "Lady, do I have to pay for this?" She quickly retorted with a smile, "Of course you have to! But never mind, I'll make it free!" I thanked her profusely and walked away from the counter.

These are the small moments of joy you experience even in a tiresome journey. My travel to Bogota and back was not for any professional reasons, but for the pleasure of the trip itself. To quote one of those beautiful words of Saint Augustine which I had religiously followed, "The world is a book and those who do not travel read only a page." Travelling has always been my passion, and I made it a point to travel at least a month in a year.

Clearing security, I picked up a hot Americano and found a cosy seat near my boarding gate, stretched my legs, and started sipping my coffee while my mind was racing back in time. I began to wonder how I became such a travel enthusiast. What was it that unleashed the desire to explore? Why, dear reader, did I choose such an expensive hobby? What was the spark that ignited me with this passion?

I didn't hail from a family of travellers. My early years as a kid were very gloomy with no playmates around. Raised in Madras (It's always Madras for me even if they have rechristened it as Chennai) at my grandmother's house, my whole world comprised of only home and school. Apart from school, the most frequented place would be the stationery store at the end of the street and the grocery stores a couple of blocks from home.

My travels in those days consisted of going to my hometown, Tadipatri in Andhra Pradesh, to visit my parents for the summer and Christmas holidays. Every October, my parents would come to Madras and, as a routine, would take me for a short vacation to Trichy, a town in Southern Tamil Nadu, India. My little sister used to accompany us. I used to wait for the holidays eagerly. We would leave my grandmother's house in the evening and go to Egmore railway station which was then a starting point for buses going south. There used to be an old restaurant at the corner opposite the railway station called Hotel Impala where we would have piping hot *dosas* before our journey. Getting out of the restaurant, we had to search for our bus to board. It was mayhem, with numerous buses all honking at the same time and the touts around trying to put you in one of those buses. Those buses were very colourful and looked like candy bars of different flavours.

Boarding the bus to Trichy, my sister and I would have a small fight to determine who gets the window seat. My sister would always win and I would have to wait for her to sleep to take my turn. Looking out of the window and feeling the gusty wind hit my face and the many lights from different vehicles blinding me, I felt happy - an unknown joy, breaking the shackles of confinement, and feeling a breath of fresh air. I used to frequently lean from my seat to look at the front glass to see how many buses we overtook. It was as though we were in a midnight race. Somewhere during midnight, the bus would halt for refreshments. My father would get down and I would follow him. While my father had a cup of tea, I would watch the driver in awe as he went around the bus, checking the tires, splashing water on the windshield, and cleaning it spic and span. I would always think about how blessed the driver was – he visits different places and enjoys life!

Arriving at Trichy, we always stayed at Hotel Ajanta. It was supposed to be a big hotel in those days. After a quick shower, my father would book a taxi and our tour of Trichy would begin. Starting with Vayaloor (the temple town of Lord Muruga), Samayapuram (the temple town of Goddess Amman), Sri Rangam (the temple town of Sri Ranganatha), and our day would end with Ucchi Pillayar Koil (also known as Malai Koil). Again, there would be the ritual of fighting my sister for occupying the front seat of the car. Finally, it would be my father in the front with my sister on his lap. Before going to each temple, my sister and I would collect ten paise coins and fill our pockets just to give it to the mendicants sitting outside the temples. There would be a good-natured rush between us to give them out fast. The next day, we would return to Madras and I was back to my mundane world. This routine travel repeated for many years yet the experience of joy was new each time.

My first solo journey happened when I was around twelve years of age. It was the Christmas holidays, if I remember correctly. As there was no one to accompany me to Tadipatri, my hometown, I was allowed to travel alone. There was this train called the Dadar Express which started from Madras Central to Bombay. It would start at around 9:30 AM in the morning and would reach Tadipatri at about 5 PM in the evening. My grandmother dropped me off at the station and warned me time and again not to get down at any station before the destination. A family going to Bombay took guardianship. It was their duty to see to it that I got down safely at my hometown. I still remember vividly. I had a packet of lemon rice with crispy potato fries for lunch and a bottle of water. Since it was the first time I was travelling on my own, the experience was thrilling, and I felt like an adult. I took out my notebook and started writing all the station names which passed by.

Being an introvert, I hardly spoke with my co-passengers. My day's journey went holding the windowsill and peering out to see the telephone poles pass by and counting the bridges and waiting for a train to pass in the opposite direction. The booming sound and the blustery wind which accompanied the train gave an energy spike. My day's guardian told me to be ready at the door when the train was slowing down to my destination. I scrupulously followed their instructions and waited at the door. When the train reached Tadipatri, it was raining torrentially. The train would stop for no more than two minutes and, as it was raining, I was scared to get down as my grandmother would never allow me to get wet in the rain. If I did, I got my quota of thrashing. It was raining and I just stood at the door waiting for the rain to stop when a voice yelled at me. "Hey, are you getting down here?" I said, "Yes, I have to get down here. But it is raining!" With no hesitation, he said, "You idiot! Get down, or else you will have to get down at Bombay!" and he unceremoniously pushed me down. My father was there waiting for me and I rushed to hug him. A grand journey accomplished! Even today when I remember the incident, I always think "How idiotic of me to wait for the rain to stop!"

The refreshing memories of my childhood brought a smile on this tiresome day and little did I realise that there were people around me, forming a line, and getting ready to board the Turkish Airlines flight. I took my bag and joined the queue to embark on the second leg of my journey back home.

II

It was a zone-wise boarding and with further checks ahead, I stepped into the aircraft and I was welcomed by a pretty air hostess and a handsome air purser. I displayed my boarding pass and they showed the way to my seat. My memory was still fresh. I was recollecting the day when I first embarked on an international journey. "*Ayubhuwan,*" said the air hostess in Sinhalese as I stepped into the Sri Lankan Airlines. Many years have passed since but my first international trip is so deeply etched in my mind that I still vividly remember all that had happened.

It was nothing but sheer luck. I was then working at the Hyderabad International Airport, and at that time, Sri Lankan Airlines had launched their first flight to Hyderabad. I went to their launch party at one of the star hotels in the city. It was a fantastic evening where I got to listen to my childhood favourite song, *Surangani Surangani...* In the end, they asked us to drop our visiting cards for a draw and the selected ones would get three-nights-four-days to stay in Colombo with round-trip tickets. I was lucky to be chosen and I embarked on the journey the following weekend with a colleague of mine. It was an emotional moment for me to go on my first international journey. With dollops of excitement, I went through immigration, got my passport stamped, and kept looking at the seal; yes, that was my first seal on the passport! The unused passport I had taken years ago with hidden ambitions, and had turned yellow at the edges, was finally being used. Boarding the flight, I felt like the kid on the bus, rushing to get the window seat. I never took my eyes off the view outside even though it was just a plain blue sea all the way.

Landing in Colombo, I checked in at Hotel Ceylon, a sea-facing hotel. The beach was immaculate and the sea pristine. The same evening, I took a stroll at the beach, and it was then that this fateful incident happened. Opposite the beach was an old colonial-style building. The lofty columns and the sandstone colour made the edifice stand majestic. I was so taken by the architecture of the building that I had to take pictures. While my friend was busy at the beach, I walked towards the monument, which I read was the Old Parliament Building. I promptly became busy taking pictures from different angles trying to put all my amateur photographic skills to use when a steady hand caught hold of my shoulder.

I turned around to see a tall army officer. He picked me up like a chicken and took me to a quiet corner of the building. Here, he made me sit in a chair, and within minutes, three more army guys joined him. They started questioning why I was here and what was I doing. I explained to them that I was a tourist from India and it was my first visit to Colombo. They didn't seem to buy that, and after fifteen minutes, another officer came and started asking the same questions for which my answers remained essentially the same.

Meanwhile, my friend was getting worried and started looking around for me. My interrogation continued for another hour and none of them were ready to accept what I was saying. I was so flustered; I forgot the name of the hotel I was staying in where I had deposited my passport.

There was some respite only after a senior officer arrived. After making a few calls, he corroborated my story with the facts. Later, he opened my camera, stripped the film roll, and asked me to go back to my hotel. Well, I couldn't blame them for their behaviour. At that time, Sri Lanka was under the grip of terrorism and their precautions were justified. To this day, I don't have a single photograph of that fateful trip.

Recollecting the memories of those days, I was rambling along the aisle when I was stopped by the crew, who showed me my seat with a gentle smile. I noticed a sexy young woman in the aisle with heavy baggage and I tried the old rope trick of offering to stow it for her. She smiled and declined the offer. She had probably seen many of my ilk. I gave her a wry smile and moved on chastened.

Mine was a window seat with ample space to stretch my legs and it was a real blessing. All thanks to the lady at the counter! I stowed my bag in the overhead cabin and sat down to relax. As the flight was getting filled up, I was praying that the seat next to me remain vacant so that I could still eke out a little more space. My prayers went unanswered – a young lady along with an elderly lady came and claimed their seats. The young lady had a wedding gown neatly packed with her and was desperately looking for a place to stow it in comfortably. With the help of the cabin crew, she was able to find a place for the bridal outfit. Once she occupied the seat next to me, I greeted her, "Hi there! How are you?" to kick off a conversation. She replied courteously, and my next question was, "Well, where you guys are headed to?" She retorted, "Why? Are you going to stalk us?" I was shocked, never expecting a question to my question as a reply. I just said, "Yeah! I would love to stalk you guys, but unfortunately, I have a flight to catch at Istanbul." She cackled off immediately, and we introduced ourselves with the necessary pleasantries. For the next fourteen hours, we talked intercepted only by interspersed sleeping.

Now that the ladies sitting next to me dozed off for a short nap, I pulled up my monitor, which was attached to the side of the seat, and started scrolling looking for movies. A movie buff that I was, it was not a surprise for me to find that I had watched most of the films, so I started to scroll through other entertainment stuff when an air hostess approached me and asked to shut the monitor as the flight was about to take off. I slid the monitor to its original place and closed my eyes. My mind again whizzed back to the old days when I used to travel to places just to watch movies! Sounds crazy, doesn't it?

I was in college, when I rented a small room for myself as my grandmother, who had raised me, had passed away. The freedom of being alone was like opium to me. As a kid, I never had the privilege of movement as my grandmother was a strict lady and never let me lay a foot on the street without her permission. All day and night, I was only supposed to study and that too aloud, so that she could hear that I was studying! I was now a free bird in my small room and it quickly became a den for friends to smoke and drink. It was then that I met a friend in my college called Mathivanan (Mathi as I would call him) who, in those days, used to go on bicycle trips to various places. He later became a close friend and my travel companion. Back then, I was a bonafide movie buff. I used to wear clothes like movie stars; my hair was styled like my favorite movie heroes - my gait, my talk, my body language, were all cinematic. Our craziness knew no bounds as we planned short trips to Tirupati in Andhra Pradesh just to watch Telugu movies. It wouldn't be an exaggeration if I say that we would watch a minimum of five films in two days! Sounds insane, right? This addiction sweetened our travels further.

After college, I got busy studying for competitive exams to land a government job. My zeal for travel was so much that for every review, I picked exam centres far from Madras so that we could explore the towns and also watch our favourite movies. In the process, I wrote my exams in various cities like Kurnool, Tirupati, Hyderabad, etc. The joy was in the travel itself. Mathi always accompanied me to these places although he did not have to appear for the exams. We took late night buses after a couple of beers and kept talking all the way and got down on frequent halts to smoke. Once we reached the destination, my first job was to locate the exam centre and then go on to explore the city. After lunch, it would be a movie, and after the film, we would crash in a local bar for a couple of drinks before going to bed. The next day, as a sincere person, I would go and write the exam. Though I shouldn't boast but I cleared all the reviews I appeared for and was lucky to land a Government job in Hyderabad.

I truly miss those days of travel. Those travels had no particular purpose, no seeking of truth; it was just the sheer joy of travelling, being in a new environment, meeting new people, and the thrill of being in a different place. It was these small ventures to the unknown, which took me to another level of excitement.

During my initial days in Hyderabad, I started missing the journeys I took with my friend, Mathi. He found a job down south, and there was little communication with him. Life started to become monotonous and boring. It was then that I decided to do something different. On one fateful Saturday at 6 AM, I went to the railway station at Secunderabad and bought a ticket to Bhopal, a city in Central India. With just two hundred rupee notes in my pocket, I boarded the Express train in the general compartment. Hardly finding a seat, I had to sit on the floor of the train. My trousers were soiled, and my journey was not comfortable. When a station would approach, I would feel hopeful of getting a seat; but before I could spot one, there would be a group ready to pounce on it. So my place remained confined to the floor throughout the journey. Though there was discomfort, there was this exhilarating sense of amusement in observing people talk amid the smell of *beedi* cigarettes and experiencing the travel of a poor common man. Yes, those were the days when people were allowed to smoke in coaches. With the little money in my pocket, I was thrifty and decided to skip lunch. Seeing me not eat anything, a Marathi family who was having lunch next to me offered me their food even as I tried to refuse politely. Eating food shared by others, sitting on the floor of a general compartment, was a different experience altogether. The food sated my hunger; the experience satiated my mental craving.

It was around 10 PM in the night when the train finally reached Bhopal. I got down with my soiled clothes smelling of hard dirt - the metallic smell which was very much a property right of the Railways. I found a water fountain on the platform and washed my face and head. Having cleaned myself partially, I walked out of the station to check the timings for my return train to Hyderabad. I learned that my train was at 4 AM in the morning and I had six hours at my disposal. I purchased my return ticket and had very little money with me. To kill time, I walked around the adjoining streets of the station, filled with eateries and tea shops, all doing brisk business with people scurrying and flocking those joints. I made my way to one of the eateries and had *roti* or the Indian bread and some curry. I then moved back to my platform waiting for the train to arrive. Though my mind was fresh and active, my body was craving rest. I found a bench in a dark corner of the platform and tried to sleep. Within seconds I was combating the mosquitoes. They were looking for a vulnerable place to pierce me, and I with my senses alert was, trying to kill the audacious ones.

Just next to me in the corner, a few mendicants were forming a circle and smoking tobacco with poppy leaves. I kept staring at them. One of them invited me to join in. With no hesitation, I went and sat with the group, not minding the soiling of my trousers. Seeing me struggle to speak Hindi, one of them asked me if I was from the south. I said, "Madras". They all joined in unison to welcome me. It was a sense of initiation into a cult group. They then started to explain that they had started from Rishikesh, and after visiting Kurukshetra and other religious places, they were now heading to Thiruvannamalai in Tamil Nadu. I was awestruck to see these people who were great travellers, travelling in search of divine truth.

I got drawn into their stories and was peppering them with questions about the Himalayas. They said, "Son, we can never explain the grandeur of the Himalayas. You have to experience it." One of them invited me to join their smoking session. I was a bit scared, and I said, "No, sir, I am scared. I do smoke cigarettes, but this, I am scared," and I refused. The eldest one in the group questioned, "If you are scared to take this small puff, how on earth are you going to experience the Himalayas? Try it, kid!" Now that they scratched me and put a wedge in my mind, I thought, well, there is no harm in trying, and again it's just a small puff. I said, "Sir, pass it on to me!" The eldest one in the group took the short pipe and started filling it with dried leaves and tobacco which he secured in a piece of cloth tightly wound around his waist. He then took a small piece of wet cloth, put it at the end of the pipe, and lit the other end. He said, "Son! Just say '*Jai Shambo Shankar*!' and take a deep drag." With equal parts of trepidation and excitement, I took the pipe, and with all my strength, I dragged it deep into my lungs, and before I could finish saying "Jai..." I croaked and coughed out and I was just an inch short of vomiting. The whole group broke into laughter seeing my agony. Again the eldest one chipped in and said, "Take it slow kid, you seem to be in a hurry to know things!" This time I smoked it like a cigarette, and after a few puffs, I could feel myself floating lightly. It was a feeling that made me look at my surroundings as a heap of stupidity and me being the only intelligent one! My throat felt dry and I told the group that I am off to sleep. I thanked them for the joyous moment I was experiencing and walked to the nearby water fountain, filled myself with as much water as possible, and dozed off on the adjacent railway platform bench. I was in a deep slumber when I heard a distant voice telling me, "Sir! Get up your train has come!" I opened my eyes. I found the air hostess beside me asking, "Sir, would you care for a drink?" "Oh, yes!" I said and picked a small bottle of red wine.

III

My fellow travellers stirred out of their naps and grabbed for themselves a large whiskey each. We started having our drinks with a packet of fried nuts to munch. I could always do with another one.

I looked at the lady next to me and asked, "So you are getting married! Congratulations!"

She laughed and said, "Oh no! Probably you got this idea seeing the bridal dress didn't you? We are going to attend my sister's wedding in Chişinău, Moldova. She got the gown stitched in the US and we are carrying it for her."

"Wow! A European venue and an American costume! That should be a great wedding!" I said with a grin on my face.

"No! It's not an Indian wedding where you celebrate for a week." the elder lady quipped.

"No! That's for the rich folks. A common man's wedding is just a one-day affair!"

"So your wedding was for how many days?" She paused a bit and asked, "I guess you are married, aren't you?"

I took a deep breath and with a sigh said, "I was once married but not anymore. My wedding was a one-day celebration, and later, it ended in a disaster!"

Both the ladies were looking at me intently and I could see the contrite in their eyes that they had picked up a wrong theme to discuss. To lighten up, I raised my wine and said, "To tranquility and peace post-marriage!" "Well, if it is so, yeah! To tranquility and peace!" and they raised a toast. Now they did feel some relief and the discussion moved on. Yet to satisfy her curiosity, the elderly lady moved again to the topic of marriage. She tried to put in as many polite words as possible to extract more information. She asked, "Well, you seem to be a nice person, and in India, I guess the family takes the responsibility of finding a nice girl. Where do you think things went wrong?" The young lady was looking at her in dismay and motioned with her eyes to not dig deep into this.

I sensed the situation and shot back. "It is okay. I don't feel bad or reluctant to discuss. I have long back moved on. Well, to answer you," I continued, "it is true that the families arrange most marriages in India. It is usually a marriage between families, between wealth, and between castes. But a marriage of hearts is sheer luck. Some are lucky to find their soul mates in an arranged marriage. Some just compromise and blame their situation on fate or *karma* and adjust with reality. In the process, they create an illusion of happiness. Some uncompromising few like me feel it is best to separate and lead a life of their choice. So it has its pros and cons. At least we do not pass on the poison to the kids in a toxic relationship."

"What is important is that you stay happy," the elderly woman concluded. "Yeah, you are right. The purpose of life is to be happy and not to reel in sorrow. It is not that my ex is a bad woman or that I am a saint. The only reason was incompatibility. Maybe her life would have been better had she married someone akin to her likings and the same goes for me."

"True! True!" both of them nodded their heads in approval. I said, "Well, I think I will just close my eyes for a bit and get ready for another round of wine." The ladies laughed and said, "Yeah! It's been four hours now, and I think we better walk to the back and stretch ourselves lest we should feel cramped." And they both walked the aisle to the end of the aircraft.

Though I said that I had moved on, it was always sad to remember the things which had led to the separation. It wasn't a comfortable situation to handle. The moment I realised that my family was no more with me, the whole world around me collapsed. All the while, I thought I had a purpose in life – to take care of and nurture the family. Now that was all gone. I had twin daughters. It was a pleasure to see them grow and now that opportunity was gone. It was not a peaceful separation but rather a prolonged, tedious, ruthless, and a protracted process which took years. I was in solitude and this loneliness broke my spirit and I was clueless and directionless in life.

It was then these two things happened. A friend of mine gave me a piece of advice. He asked me to go to a Government Hospital and take a walk in the burns ward and return. Heeding to his idea, I went to the Kilpauk Medical College Hospital, Madras, located the burns ward and took a slow walk watching the sad situation there. I saw people with maximum burns being laid on the floor with no beds and covered with nothing but banana leaves. Their faces were disfigured and their families were sitting and tending to them. There was a stench of burnt skin all over the place. I couldn't walk further and had to return. I took a moment of my time to contemplate the problems of those in the hospital. How miserable life would be for the person if he survives? And if he dies, what would happen to the family? What sort of problems would have driven a person to torch himself? All these questions and thoughts occupied my mind the whole day. It then dawned on me how blessed I was! This incident made me accept the reality of life and made me look forward to what was in store. The next one was like a soothing balm for my wounds.

My cousin, Raja, who lives in Malaysia, invited me to stay with him believing that a trip to Malaysia would be a change of scenery and would help me in my mental recovery. I took a month off and reached Kuantan in Malaysia, his hometown, and stayed with him. In the evenings, I would either accompany him to the local club for a drink or would go to the beach and sit and watch the South China Sea sending wave after wave to hit the shores. My cousin then booked tickets for me and asked me to go and explore South East Asia on my own. He made a few calls to his friends residing in various countries to help me in case of any need. I was not ready to move around. All I needed was seclusion. My mind was blank and my cognitive process was at its lowest. I walked around just like another zombie.

With persuasion and reluctance, I boarded my flight to Sabah, a region on an island to the east of Malaysia called Borneo. I landed at Kota Kinabalu, the capital. I checked in at a nondescript local hotel. Having no interest in anything, I stayed put in the hotel room for the whole day. I got a call from Raja inquiring about me, and with some cajoling and prodding from his side, I decided to go out and take a stroll. I walked through the Filipino fishermen colonies, the local markets, and the local food joints where they sold local delicacies. Feeling famished, I stopped at one of the local eateries and asked the vendor to give me some food. He handed over a plate of soft-shelled crabs. With no interest to pamper my palate, I started to eat, and to my surprise, it was so divine and so soft that it melted in my mouth. Lost interests began to rear their heads out. I ordered some more, and with a sense of satisfaction, I left the place. Probably the saying is true, "The way to a man's heart is through his stomach."

The next day, I felt a little better and thought of exploring the beauty of Borneo. I visited the wildlife park, which had beautiful wildlife like the pygmy elephants and the proboscis monkeys, well known for their promiscuity. I bought a book from the zoo to learn more about these species. From Sabah, I flew to Miri in Sarawak, also a part of Borneo. Miri was a centre for oil extraction and my cousin Raja joined me as he had to visit for business purposes. Sarawak has a majority of Christians, which is in stark contrast with the predominant Muslims in the Malaysian straits. I did nothing there but just spent my time enjoying the local bars. Men would be strumming their guitars and playing country numbers and I would be in a deep trance listening to them. There were moments when I became emotional. My eyes would brim with tears, especially when listening to the song *Sacrifice* by Elton John which kindled my deepest emotions.

My next visit was to Bandung in Indonesia. Slowly I could sense myself getting out of the misery I allowed my life to put me in. I now felt the need to get out, meet people, explore the unknown, and try the untried. Feeling fresh the next morning, I started to traverse the city. This city was known for two things, one, Mount Sunda, which is a volcano, and two, for the cheap clothing outlet stores. I took a local taxi and went up to the crater of Mount Sunda. It was a massive bowl with air full of the stench of sulphuric acid. There were shops up to the crater selling all sorts of curios. I walked around the place for an hour and then from there, I took a cab and went to Jakarta, the capital of Indonesia. It is one of the busiest cities in the world. I never had the mood to visit tourist sites but preferred to take long walks along the alleys and eat at small roadside joints. For the next two days, I trudged across Jakarta.

From Jakarta, it was Manila, Philippines. I stayed in a local hostel in the heart of the city. Hostels are a beautiful place to get to know people. One gets the opportunity to interact with people from different countries and it was a delightful surprise to know that there are people who do nothing but travel for years together. I formed a group with two Israelis, a German, and a Swede. We went around the city exploring the Intramuros – a walled city within the town of Manila, Fort Santiago, and the vast Rizal Park. In Manila, we tried tasting the famous Filipino delicacy of Balut – a fertilised egg embryo directly eaten from the shell and Chicken Adobo – which resembles the regular chicken rice but cooked in the local Filipino way. I, as usual, relished both; but my friends from the hostel couldn't appreciate the food, especially the Balut. The next day I bid adieu to my new friends and took a local bus to a town called Tagaytay. I stayed in a room facing the famous Taal volcano. The cool breeze from the lake on the volcano was very refreshing. In the afternoons, I would walk up to the people's park in the sky – a historical urban park, and in the evenings, I would visit the local karaoke clubs listening to the Filipinos sing. The Filipinos seem to be great fans of karaoke as I could see there are numerous karaoke bars in the town. After spending a couple of days there, I flew to Singapore to visit my sister.

Things were slowly returning to normal and the stay with my sister in Singapore gave me the required confidence and assurance that there are people who still care for me and are ready to support me. After spending a couple of days in Singapore, I flew to Ho Chi Minh City or Saigon in Vietnam. From Ho Chi Minh, I took a hydrofoil to reach Vung Tau, a neighboring city, to join my cousin Raja who had come for a business trip. While he was busy at work, I started my exploration by first visiting the Statue of Jesus Christ. This one resembles Christ the Redeemer of Rio de Janeiro. Facing the sea, there was this colossal statue where one could climb up inside, exit standing next to the chin of Christ and have a panoramic view of the majestic sea. From there, I went to the food street to taste local Vietnamese delicacies and the famous Vietnam coffee. My cousin flew off to Malaysia from Vietnam and I took a flight to Siem Reap in Cambodia.

In Siem Reap, or the city of Angkor Wat, I came face to face with the splendour and the greatness of the human mind in the field of architecture. Never ever in my life would I see such a marvellous temple structure that I saw that day! Sprawling over 400 acres, it was a vast Hindu temple. Though now in ruins, it is a World Heritage site. It took me a whole day to just look at those structures. The Indian influence on the temple architecture is startling. Thanks to Angelina Jolie's movie *The Tomb Raider,* many became aware of this phenomenal spectacle on earth. It truly deserves a place among the Wonders of the World.

People who know history do know that Cambodia was under the tyrannical rule of the Khmer Rouge in the 1970s. There is this museum in Siem Reap which displays collections from the Pol Pot era. I visited the museum to enrich my knowledge about Cambodian history. There I found a big rectangular pillar. It was about six feet in height and I was shocked to see the box filled with human skulls. The memorabilia of the massacre was on a naked display. It was indeed a symbol of shame for humanity where humans throughout history have proven that they were no better than savage animals. At least animals live by instinct; we should be ashamed to say that we live by reason. Cambodian history is an example of the opposite attributes of humankind. On the one hand, we see human brilliance exhibited through the constructions of the temples of Angkor Wat. On the other, we see the shameful display of the callous, brutal, and heartless animal instinct displayed in those killing fields.

After Cambodia, my next stop was Chiang Rai in Thailand. The northernmost city of Thailand lies on the bank of the Kok River, a tributary of the Mekong River. This city forms a part of the Golden Triangle bordering Burma, Laos, and Thailand. This area is also well known for opium cultivation. At Chiang Rai, I hired a boat that would take me to Burma, where there was a small casino to gamble and lose, and from there to Laos and back to Thailand. At Laos, I got off the boat and walked for an hour visiting the local Laos village. Here, I had the enjoyable experience of having snake whiskey. There were these large jars of local alcohol and in them were snakes with their hoods open. Some even had a scorpion in their mouth. They offered me a glass of this whiskey free of cost and said it was an excellent aphrodisiac. Closing my nose, I gulped the whole glass in one go. It tasted awful and I felt my head spin for a moment. I picked one bottle, thanked them for the experience, and got back on my boat to Chiang Rai and back to Malaysia.

They say time heals, but travel quickens the process. A couple of months earlier, I felt that I had lost the purpose of life. Life was gloomy and depressing. I felt each passing day meant a day closer to the grave. I was struggling to escape from the naked reality. During the South East Asian travel, I was alone to confront my demons. It was a time for introspection, a time to realise how my problems were minuscule when compared with those of others, especially the people of Cambodia. My walks in the alleys of Jakarta and other cities made me see the state of affairs of people who struggle for their daily living whereas I was in a much more comfortable position. I had always considered my social circle and life to be the most crucial thing in the world. This travel shattered the myth I was holding on to and Nature had given me glimpses of its vitality, grandeur, and variety, challenging me to discover it and connect with it. Returning to Malaysia, life was not the same. I was a transformed person who accepted the reality of life and was ready to move forward and explore. Life, at times, passes through rough weather, but there is always tranquility afterwards.

"Sir, we are passing through rough weather, please straighten your seat and fasten your seat belt," the air hostess announced. Yes, the rough weather will be short-lived, and then there will be tranquility.

IV

After a few minutes, the seat belt sign was switched off. I stood up and stretched myself. The young lady next to me said, "I am going to get a drink, do you need one?" I said, "Yes! Please get me a whiskey." "Oh, sure." she said and walked towards the pantry and quickly returned with three glasses. We toasted, and as a habit, I held the glass in my hand and closed my eyes for a few seconds. When I opened my eyes, both the ladies were inquisitively staring at me, and the young lady lost no opportunity to ask, "Were you praying?" I replied with a smile, "No, I wasn't. I just thanked God for the drink." "Thanking God for a drink? You thank God for your vices?" Both the ladies were looking at me unbelievingly. I said, "Yes, what is wrong in thanking God for the drink? There are millions of people in the world who can't afford water, and here I am so blessed to have a whiskey in the sky! Shouldn't I thank my Maker?" I then continued, "Drinking is never a vice. Anything taken in excess is a vice. Just like in Christianity, eating is not a sin, but gluttony is, isn't it?" The ladies nodded their heads as if they were satisfied with the answer for now but would be ready to draw swords later when they get reasons enough to crucify me.

I started sipping and the warmth of the whiskey filled my throat. The elderly lady bent forward and asked, "Well, I guess you are a Hindu, right?" and before I could answer, she concluded that I was a Hindu. She continued further, "So tell me, you guys have a lot of Gods, do you pray to all the Gods or you get to choose one and pray to the one you chose."

I smiled at her and started to explain. Both the ladies stopped sipping their drinks and focused all their attention on me as though expecting a revelation. I said, "The concept that there are many Gods in Hinduism is a farfetched one. We believe in a supreme God and that supreme God encompasses all the living and non-living things. So we see God in living things like a tree, an animal, a human, and we also see God in non-living things like a stone, lake, mountain, fire. You name it, we see God in it. That's the reason we find many temples dedicated to stones, trees, and other things. First, it is not Hinduism but rather called *Sanathana Dharma*. It is just a way of life. There are no strict rules to follow. There are no dos and don'ts. You can be a theist or an atheist or an agnostic and still be in the *Sanathana* fold. Your salvation is in your hands and it is up to you how you make it. I could probably put it in simpler words. The oldest religion of the world has four *Vedas*, eighteen *Puranas*, two epics, one hundred and eight *Upanishads*, and numerous commentaries. The concept, at times, is not comprehensible to a common man. So the ideas are depicted in a pictorial form for common understanding. For example, we see God with many hands; it does not mean that God is multi-handed. It is just to emphasise the fact that God is powerful and is capable of doing many things. This depiction has led to many Gods and Goddesses."

"That was quite an explanation. If my guess is right, you must be a student of Theology," the lady next to me quipped with her eyes beaming as though she had discovered the undiscovered.

I said, "No way! I am neither a student of Theology nor a religious person. Based on my understanding, it appears to be the truth, but who knows!"

In my mind, I was grinning like a Cheshire cat when I heard the comment that I could be a student of Theology when, on the contrary, I was once an atheist! My thoughts again took me back to my college days when I was drawn to the works of Ayn Rand, and it was my friend, Mathi, who introduced me to the writings of Ayn Rand and Objectivism. We used to firmly believe that everything had to stand the test of reason. Our thoughts and ideas were firmly and deeply rooted in the philosophical premise of Ayn Rand, "Existence is Identity; Consciousness is Identification." God was never accepted as he failed the test of reason. This knowledge of Objectivism, which I gained through voracious reading, gave me a tinge of arrogance. It wasn't long before I accepted the fact that where science and reason ends, the realm of belief starts. It was again my travels - the religious ones, which brought about the transformation.

My first religious travel was not for the love of God but for the thrill of trekking. It was a journey to Amarnath – a Hindu shrine located in Jammu and Kashmir, India, at the height of 12,750 ft. The

Government organised the trek and there were rigorous security checks as the place was always a target for terrorists. I was in a convoy of 150 buses piloted by a military escort with machine guns mounted on the vans. Once the buses started their journey, I couldn't believe my eyes; there were people outside cheering us. The passengers in the bus shouted slogans in praise of Lord Shiva and the sound was deafening. On the roadside, atop buildings were men, women, and children cheering us and some immersed in a silent prayer for our well-being. All these prayers and cheering gave me a sense of bliss and I realised that my eyes were wet with tears. This was probably the first time I recognised and felt the power of belief. All along the way, soldiers were deployed at intervals of not more than a hundred yards.

For say every five miles or so, there was a group of military personnel with all the defence paraphernalia providing security. We winded up each day in makeshift tents and spent the chilly nights cocooned in blankets. There were nights when I slept in a stable. Our trek route went through Pissu Top via Sheshnag, which is about 12,000 ft above sea level, covering a distance of 12 km. The walk was very strenuous and I nearly collapsed on my way before a co-trekker gave me some glucose water. With intermittent rest, I walked further, and the more I walked, the destination seemed to go further away from me. At that time, I remember a *sadhu* or a hermit, who came to me and said, "Child, don't look at the destination. Look at your footsteps. That will take you to your goal." What he said was right as it applies to our day to day life also.

The weather was frigid but with determination, I pushed myself throughout the journey. The second-day trek was 18 km, and when I reached a place called Mahaguna Top, which was 15,000 ft above sea level, I experienced pangs from lack of oxygen, and a piece of camphor came in handy as smelling it relieved me. The day ended at Panchtarni. The next day was a steep climb of five km and an additional one km walk on ice, and quite naturally, I loved the latter. On reaching Amarnath, I decided to have a bath and took a plunge in the brook where the water was icy cold. At one point, I felt I was dead and was starting to freeze. My fingers began aching. It felt like a thousand sharp nails piercing me from all directions. It took some time to get back to normalcy and once warmness crept in, I continued my walk towards the holy cave.

At an altitude of around 12,000 ft, this cave is a famous Hindu shrine that is snow-clad for most of the year except for a short period in summer when it is open for pilgrims. Devotees consider the stalagmite formed due to the freezing of water drops that fall from the roof as a *Shiv Ling* – an iconic representation of the Hindu deity Shiva. Inside the cave, I was like a drop of water in an ocean. There was a stampede like situation as the arrangements were not up to the mark. Having reached the cave at 10:30 AM, I kept swaying with the crowd until 2:30 PM. With tremendous effort, I jumped over the fence and entered inside. There was a massive rush and it was suffocating. I was aware that a person had died the day before due to a lack of oxygen. With too many people around, the *Shiv Ling* had reduced drastically from 7 feet to

3 feet. People prayed to their God and collected the water droplets coming from the *ling* in small containers; some started digging the cave for holy ashes. There was a mad rush to take something, anything, from the cave rather than indulging in silent prayer. Well, people pray to God, but they forget to find the reason as to why one has to pray. I did observe that people gave more importance to the sacred things attached to God than God *per se*.

This journey gave me my first interaction with Nature. I was in total awe of the pristine power of Nature. I started to see and believe how minuscule I was and how my knowledge and the false bloated ego was not even a matter of consideration in front of its vastness. This journey gave me an inkling of my relationship with Mother Nature.

A few years later, I had the opportunity to embark on another religious trekking trip. The destination was to Tibet via the Himalayas. This time it was for the thrill of trekking and the joy of interacting with Nature. My earlier trip to Amarnath had shown me a glimpse of how it would be in the lap of Mother Nature. Now I was ready to experience it in full. This trip was a month-long trek, so there were rigorous health checkups and screenings to ascertain if a person was fit to undertake the journey. After the initial selections, a group of 47 people, including me, were selected for the trek. It was a three day bus journey up to the foothills of the Himalayas to a village named Mangti, and from there, we had to start the trek. Some took ponies and others walked. The route from Mangti to Buddhi was a picturesque one with lush greenery on one side and the roaring river Kali on the other side. The roar of the river was very loud at times.

Walking through the paths carved out from the rocks in the mountains was an enjoyable experience. As the stones were slippery, we had to walk with utmost caution. At specific points, I had to walk through waterfalls and getting drenched was quite an experience in itself. The camp at Buddhi (8,990 ft) was like an igloo-like room that could accommodate around 8 to 12 people. A mattress and a quilt were all I needed to doze off.

Mornings were very fresh with the cool breeze blowing and I could notice a change in the weather. We started off trekking to Gunji, covering a distance of 18 km. The first five km was a treacherous walk along a steep path. Once crossed, it was a smooth walk through Chialekh, a spectacular valley and home for rare mountain flowers like Cobra flowers, Irises, Mayapple flowers, *Kasturikamal,* etc. Walking through the beautiful green meadow, we reached Garbyang, also known as the sinking village, a geologically blighted ground with weak shale moorings; large houses have now slid down to the level of the river.

After passing through a blanket of aromatic trees, we saw the confluence of the Kali and Tinker rivers with the Tinker hurtling away into Nepal. The day's trek ended at Gunji village, which was at the height of 11,485 ft.

It was here that I had a horrible experience. It must be around 11 PM when all of us were fast asleep and I started to feel breathless. I suddenly woke up and saw myself sweating and panting for breath. I was sleeping with eight others in a bunker, and with the high altitude and people around me, there was less oxygen. This made it all the more difficult. I had a weird thought that I had an attack, and I started crying, thinking that those were my last few moments. I immediately rushed out of the bunker and started taking deep breaths. The weather outside was icy chill but very comfortable compared to inside the shelter. I spent around half an hour outside and then went in and opened a small window so that air could circulate. After a while, I felt better though not completely alright. It had been a difficult night to pass. We had to stay in Gunji for a couple of days so that our bodies could acclimatise to the extreme weather conditions.

From Gunji, our trek took us to Lipuleh pass (17,500 ft), traversing Kalapani and Navidang. It was a beautiful stretch to walk along with the beautiful Kali River on one side and the gorgeous mountains on the other side. The path from Kalapani to Navidang was an arduous uphill climb. As we proceeded, we left behind the river Kali, and we saw lesser and lesser vegetation on the way. At Navidang, one could see the Om Parvat - a mountain, which has the Sanskrit "Om" written on it in snow. Since the weather was terrific, the trek from Navidang to Lipuleh pass was a treacherous one for those who preferred to walk. As we kept going, we could see that there was no vegetation and the land was barren. At the height of 16,500 ft, the oxygen levels were low and each step became increasingly difficult. Smelling camphor helped to relieve spells of discomfort. The crossing of the pass was a finely timed affair with the group entering into Tibet meeting the exiting group. The timing was perfect and we didn't have to wait as the Chinese authorities were there by the time we reached. From Lipuleh, it was a downhill trek of seven km which put tremendous strain on my thighs and calf muscles. Getting down from a height of 17,500 ft all of a sudden, brought on a terrible headache.

At the foothill, there was a bus ready to take us to Taklakot, a nearby town. It is a small Tibetan town which was once an ancient trading post. There were a few Nepali restaurants where I, along with a few friends, would go for lunch to taste some spicy food as the food served at our designated stay was too bland to eat. Moreover, another thing which I observed was that since Tibet lies in the same longitude as India, the sunrise and sunset timings are more or less the same. But since China, as a country, follows the Beijing Standard Time throughout the nation, which is two and a half hours ahead of India, sunrise in Tibet would be around 8:30 AM IST. People start to work and children go to school even before sunrise as they follow the time in Beijing. Likewise breakfast was served at around 5:30 AM IST which is 8 AM Tibet or China time.

After spending a couple of days in Taklakot, we started our onward journey. We boarded a bus to a place called Qihu by the Manasarovar Lake. We were a batch of 27 people for Manasarovar and the rest 20 for Kailash. The route was through a dusty road with no vegetation in sight but only sand all the way. Our first halt was the Rakshas Tal (14,815 ft). It was a beautiful and spectacular lake. Looking at the lake, I was spellbound. It was as though I was staring at a painting. A mere glance at the lake was worth the pain of coming all the way from India. Unlike Manasarovar, Hindus do not revere this lake. People compare Manasarovar to the light of the day and Rakshas

Tal to the darkness of night. Rakshas Tal finds mention in the famous Hindu epic, the *Ramayana*. Ravana, the demon king of Lanka, the antagonist in the sacred Sanskrit epic, is said to have meditated on the shores of Rakshas Tal to seek Lord Shiva's favour. It is from here that we get to see the first view of Mount Kailash. We stayed for the night at Qihu.

Once the weather was warm, I proceeded to take a dip in the Manasarovar Lake. The beauty of the lake is that it changes colour and mood with the passing hours and seasons - placid now, furious the next. The reflection of the sun, the clouds, the stars, and even Kailash, keeps the beholder spellbound. Its fascinating variety and beauty captures the heart and imagination of the viewers. The water of the lake can be freezing at certain times of the day and pleasantly warm at other times.

It was an enjoyable experience as the water was just the right amount of cold and a dip made me feel refreshed. It was as though I got a new lease of life. After our trip around the lake, we proceeded to Darchan, a town in Tibet, to continue our journey to Mount Kailash.

From Darchan, we reached a place called Yamadwar, a site believed to be the abode of Lord *Yama*, the God of death. From this point on, we were on a trek to go around Mount Kailash, which took us three whole days of trekking to complete. Along the way, we passed magnificent rock cliffs with streams and falls flowing through some of them. Some even had Buddhist mantras inscribed on them. We retired for the night at Dherapuk, from where we had the closest and brightest view of Mount Kailash. The view of the Kailash is so mesmerising that it even makes an atheist raise his hands in supplication.

Mount Kailash, at an altitude of 22,028 ft, is regarded by Hindus, Buddhists, Jains, and the followers of the Bon religion as the centre of the spiritual world. Its peak, which is always snow-clad, is said to have holy vibrations. They believe that one circumambulation around Kailash washes away your past sins, while a 108 could be your ticket to nirvana. It was here for the first time I saw snowfall in my life. From Dherapuk, the journey becomes treacherous, with the oxygen levels getting lower and lower as we gain height. After three hours of trekking, we reached Dolma Pass, the highest point of the circumambulation. As a measure of comparison, we were at over 19,000 ft, whereas the altitude of the base camp to Everest is only around 17,000 ft! Passing the Dolma Pass remains a test of determination and faith as chilly winds, low temperature, and even the occasional blizzards strike without warning. Breathing was getting complicated and we had to move immediately.

There was this one thing that caught my attention. I saw a Buddhist monk circumambulating by kneeling and prostrating. He was doing this throughout the way instead of walking. I was astonished by the faith people have and the amount of pain they were ready to bear when it comes to worship. Half a kilometer down is the beautiful Gaurikund Lake. The emerald green water of the lake amidst the pristine surroundings was a visual delight. The lake, at 18,400 ft, is one of the highest in the world. The water of that pond is said to have curative powers and people eagerly filled water in cans from the lake.

Completing our journey around Mount Kailash, we reached Darchan, where there was bad news awaiting us. One of the travellers from our group, unable to cope up with the weather, expired of pulmonary edema. It was a shock to us. We performed the funeral and last rites at Darchan as carrying his body to India would have been impossible. From Darchan, we reached Taklakot and from there to Lipuleh pass and entered India. Setting foot back in our motherland was such an incredible feeling that words are inadequate. It was like landing back in safe hands. The feeling that I was being taken care of throughout every step of mine felt reassuring. In China, the fear of death had haunted me throughout as I felt that anything could happen with the vagaries of climate and the fact that no one was there for me. To top it off, we witnessed the death of one of our fellow travellers. In India, such fear never existed and the fragrance in the air I breathed then still lingers in my mind. Yes, home is always sweet!

After a few days of trek and a tedious bus journey, we returned to New Delhi. The month long trip had come to an end. Everybody was eager to take the contact details of others. Some people left immediately and some went the next day, and I was again alone on my way back home but with memories that I would relish for the days to come. It was a month long journey where I was in the wild with people who I wasn't acquainted with. But by the end of the trip, I had become friends with them. This journey allowed me to meet people of a different mindsets. There was this one person who proclaimed that Shiva had given *darshan* to him along with his wife and two children Ganesh and Kartikeya. There was this other person, a well-read software professional, who was reluctant to take photographs at the Rakshas Tal, a beautiful lake as he believed that the lake emanates negative energy. A study of these people would be a psychologist's delight. All said and done, they had their reasons for their ideas, and maybe I should stand in their shoes to reason out why.

A month long trek in the wilderness with people from different parts of the country naturally had a significant impact on me. I was blessed to undertake it as it allowed me to interact with Nature, where I learned to be submissive to it. Nature unleashes before you, in extraordinary magnitude, the pristine beauty of itself; and above all, it fosters living with your own self. It puts you at various altitudes and temperatures, and at times Nature may be unkind towards you, but it is only perseverance which helps you at the end. A sound body and a sound mind are the two things that are mandatory for the trek. The tedious uphill trek and a steep downhill descent, the low oxygen levels, the cramping of 8-12 people in one bunker which suffocates, the chilly weather, the cold dip, the tanning of the skin, all these put the body to severe task. The one who is ready to take the challenge is the one destined to have the divine vision and experience. I witnessed myself transformed from an atheist to an admirer of Nature.

Well, how did this admirer of Nature become a theist? I looked into my glass; it was empty, and those ladies beside me were not there. Probably they would have gone to stretch themselves. I got up and walked to the pantry for a refill.

V

With a glass of whiskey in one hand and a packet of nuts in the other, I returned to my seat. The air hostess said that they would be serving lunch shortly. I then realised it had been nearly five hours of flying. Sitting comfortably, I pulled my tray out, kept my glass and stretched myself. I started to sip my drink leisurely, revelling in the joy of solo drinking. Though drinking alone with some lovely country music in the background is enjoyable, nothing beats having a drink with a friend involving some intense and meaningful conversation. These conversations are always there whenever I drink with my friend Mathi. It was in those days when Mathi was too engrossed with spiritualism. I remember one of the conversations which led us to start another great adventure – a religious one!

While I was working at Madras, Mathi had come down to meet and spend some days with me. As an evening ritual, we sat down with our glasses filled with our favourite whiskeys. I remember that we were discussing the latest news about a Godman caught in the act of sex with his disciple! That news was all over the TV channels. I said, "Never believe men in religious garb; they are the most dangerous. It is the want of power that these men are after and the innocence and fear of the common man are their only investment."

My friend replied, "Well, what you say is correct, but you cannot generalise. Many Godmen in the past have changed the course of religion. They paved the way for the intellectual and spiritual well-being of humanity. One corrupt person brings shame to the whole creed."

"I don't think so! Name one. Don't tell a name from the *Vedas*. All through history, we find how religion and Godmen have exploited humanity. Karl Marx was right in saying '"Religion is the opium of the people.*"

He smiled and started to explain, "What I am going to say is drawn from the history of the last thousand years. We have had great philosophers and teachers who made the essence of the religious scripts more comprehensible to the common man. Some appealed to the intellectual's mind and some appealed to a commoner's mind." He further said, "You must have heard of Shri Adishankaracharya, who propounded the theory of *Adhvaitham* or Monotheism which says 'everything is an illusion but for the one and only Supreme God who is true' and "Shri Madhwacharya, who illustrated his theory of *Dwaitham* or Dualism, which means 'God and soul are two different things and are different from each other.'" I was listening intently and he continued, "While these two *acharyas* appealed to the intellectual mind, Shrimad Ramanuja appealed to the common man. He modified the theory of Shri Adishankaracharya and propounded his philosophy of *Vishishta-Advaitham* or Qualified Monotheism, which was easily understood by the layman. It says 'God and soul, though seem to be separate, they operate as one for their love for each other'. It states that God or *Iswara,* resides in all the things – *cit* (living), and *acit* (non-living). So God resides in you, in me, in this chair, in this drink, and in this Nature as a whole. The purpose of life is to realise the relationship one possesses with the Supreme soul and to join him in unison.

In the course of our experience and through our actions, we accumulate lots of *karma.* It may be *punya* (good karma) or *paapa* (bad karma). To be united with the Supreme Soul, you have to clean your slate of both good and bad *karma,* which is next to impossible. So the only solution that rests with us is *sharanaagathi* or unconditional surrender to the Supreme. By unconditional surrender, it means giving the fruits of your labour to God, not taking pride in your achievements or blaming others for your loss. Since the Supreme God encompasses everything, there is nothing you can take pride in. Anything you discover and invent is from here, and anything you give or donate is again from here. Nothing is yours. Once you realise this, you are a step closer to be in unison with God."

I was amazed looking at him and wondering from where in high heavens he became a repository of such knowledge! Mathi further continued quoting a verse from the *Bhagavad Gita,*

"sarva-dharmān parityajya māmekaṁ
śharaṇaṁvraja
ahaṁtvāṁ sarva-pāpebhyo mokṣhayiṣhyāmi
māśhuchaḥ

It means – Lord Krishna had earlier explained to Arjuna the various means of salvation in multiple *yugas*. He then says, 'Arjuna! Keep aside all the means of Dharma to Salvation, come to me, and surrender yourself. I shall deliver you of your sins and give you salvation. Do not worry!'" He then asked me, "Don't you think you find something similar in Christianity where Lord Jesus says 'Come to me I shall deliver you to the Lord in heaven!?"

Listening intently and gathering all this information, my mind started to work as a motor correlating and comparing many things. I was a firm believer in Ayn Rand's philosophy of Objectivism. The basic premise of her philosophy was "Existence is Identity; Consciousness is Identification." To explain, a stone is a stone and it exists for real. It is for your mind to identify it as a stone. You may even identify it as a sponge, it is up to you. Whether you recognise it or not, a stone is a stone. A is A. This is an axiomatic premise of the philosophy of Objectivism, an ethical key to open all doors of knowledge. Now coming to *Vishishta-Advaitham,* it too says something similar. God exists in all living and non-living things. The key to your salvation lies in identifying. Whether you identify or not, God exists – Existence exists! Take God and put Nature; it becomes Ayn Rand's philosophy. I did see a parallel between these two philosophies and it reminded me of the title of Leonard Piekoff's book *The Ominous Parallel."* My interest in *'Vishishta-Advaitham* started to bloom. There was this urge to know more. He further said, "There are many *Vaishnava* temples which explain their existence and elucidate the concepts through stories and anecdotes. You need to visit them. They are the *Vaishnava Divya Desams* which are 108 in number; but for two, the rest are in this world. The *Vaishnava saints,* also known as *Alwars,* glorified these temples through their hymns. You need to visit those temples, learn about them, and you get a better idea of *Vaishnavism.*" I asked him, "Have you visited those?" He said, "No, I haven't. They are spread all over India, and there is one in Nepal as well." The travel animal in me woke up and I asked him immediately, "Well, why don't we start the journey?" His face bloomed and I could see the enthusiasm in his eyes. He said yes, and we started doing our homework - listing the temples geographically, working out the routes, planning our stay, and jotting out a brief history of each temple.

Our journey started the following weekend in my car. This time it was a long drive. We started early in the day, driving on the East Coast road visiting temples on the way. Near Seerghaazhi, a town close to Pondicherry, the once French colony, we had to go deep inside the village roads to a place called Thirunangur, which had a cluster of eleven temples within a radius of ten km, I guess. We took the services of a local village kid who took us to all the temples, and when a temple was locked, he would go to the priest's house, call him and get the temple opened for us to pray. By midday, we finished visiting those temples and paid the kid for his service and continued further to visit temples in Mayavaram and Kumbakonam.

Kumbakonam is a city of temples. Apart from the numerous *Shaivite* temples, there were around eleven *Divya Desam* temples in and around the town. The priests in those temples explained to us the glory of the place and also answered our queries. It was a fast-tracked drive as we had to cover all the temples in a given time.

Driving through the muddy roads and having tea at villages was a new experience. Being food lovers, we would check out the best food joints from the locals and try out the food, whatever be the ambience, as we were just after good taste.

After visiting the temples in Kumbakonam, we drove further to Nagapatnam to visit the Thirunagai Divya Desam temple. The temple was closed and we found out that they would open at 4 PM. We decided to have lunch and proceeded to Nagore, which was nearby. Nagore has a famous Muslim *dargah,* also known as Syed Shahul Hameed Dargah, built over the tomb of a Sufi saint. Pilgrims belonging to different faiths visit the place. We saw the *dargah* which was by then too crowded. We were just pushed in and pushed out. With a lot of time still at our disposal, we drove to the Velankanni Mada Catholic Church built on the shore facing the Bay of Bengal. Luckily the church wasn't crowded, so we were able to swiftly enter and return. It was 4 PM, and by the time we reached the temple, it was open. We spent some time in the temple talking with the local priest and from there, we drove down to Tanjavur, again visiting temples on the way.

The next day was a drive down south to the island of Rameswaram to visit a temple called Thirupulani. It was the place where Lord Ram of the sacred Hindu epic *Ramayana,* supposedly started his journey to Sri Lanka to conquer Ravana, by building the *Sethu* Bridge. Paying our obeisance, we drove back home, visiting other temples en route.

One of the interesting temples we visited on our way back, is the Vekkali Amman Temple, a temple in a town called Uraiyoor near Tiruchirapalli. Dedicated to the Goddess Vekkaali, a form of Goddess Kali, the temple is quite famous in the south. The major feature is the absence of a roof over the sanctorum. Legend has it that people tried to construct the roof over the sanctum but was said to be burnt by the power of the Mother Goddess. The idol has its left leg placed over a demon and said to emanate high energy levels. In fact the name Vekkaali roughly translates to fiery or scorching Goddess Kali. The people of Uraiyoor see the goddess as their guardian deity. After spending sometime in the temple and learning its history, we returned back home with contentment.

This five day religious journey was just the first leg. There were many more such drives to come. I was able to visit around 40 temples, learn their history, and interact with the priests. This journey enriched my knowledge about *Sri Vaishnavism*. Each temple was different in its own way. I was spellbound when I saw the central statue of Lord Vishnu in the sleeping posture, which was so huge in Thirumeyam. Thirukoshtiyur is another temple where the structure has three floors, and at each level, the Lord gives *darshan* in lying, standing, and sitting posture respectively. It was at this temple that Shrimad Ramanuja preached the holy *ashtakshara mantra* – "*Om Namo Narayanayah*" to all people irrespective of caste and creed. This mantra, which means "The entire Universe as I feel, is just the Essence of Lord Vishnu", is sacred and said to have been taught by Vedic seers to the seekers who came to them for wisdom. It was Ramanuja who declared that even a common man could chant the mantra and attain salvation.

The thrill of travelling was always there in these drives. There were many occasions where we would be behind schedule and a few temples would be left to complete for the day. We had to drive faster and rush into the temples before the gates were closed. There were moments when we just slipped in before the closing of the gates. We had a great experience traversing the interior villages and interacting with the people. Each day was a new adventure. We could see the different cultures as we drove across the districts, a change in the way people speak, a change in the cuisine, the fertile lands in some regions, and barren lands in others.

After a month, Mathi and I started again to finish the remaining temples in Tamil Nadu. This time we started from Tirupati and drove south. In the process, we completed all the 83 *Divya Desam* temples in Tamil Nadu. We still had to visit 23 temples - 13 in Kerala, 1 in Andhra Pradesh, 1 in Gujarat, 4 in Uttar Pradesh, 3 in Uttaranchal, and 1 in Nepal. While working in Madras, I planned to fly once a month and cover the cities of Trivandrum, Cochin, Calicut, and Ahmedabad. I scheduled my temple visits by arranging a taxi beforehand which would drive me to the temples and drop me back at the airport. Another trip was with Mathi to north India and Nepal. Eventually, I covered all the temples.

There are many amusing anecdotes to narrate about our trips. Once Mathi and I took a train from Delhi and reached Haridwar station at about 4 AM in the morning. As soon as we got down, a horde of taxi drivers swarmed us offering their services to take us to Badrinath and other temples. After fixing a deal with one of the taxis, the driver took us to a nearby dingy lodge for us to take a bath and refresh so that in the meanwhile, he would go home and pack his clothes for the trip. He came back on time and first, he took us to Rishikesh, and we started our journey uphill. The taxi was probably one of the first models from the days of its invention. A rope secured the back door, and whenever there was a turn, I had to pull the cord tight so as not to let the door fly off. It was a bumpy ride across the central Himalayan Ghats. Our first stop was Devaprayag, a *Divya Desam* temple. The driver found a place to rest and we entered the temple. Within 30 minutes we were back and the taxi driver looked at us in disbelief. He said, "You were too fast. People stay here till evening and some even stay a night here!" I said, "We have no time. We need to go." We started, and by six in the evening, we reached Badrinath.

The driver put us in a lodge and said there was a massive rush in the temple, so it would be better to get up early and visit the shrine. Mathi and I had a quick shower and walked to the temple. True to what the driver said, there was a long queue, and probably it would have taken hours to enter the temple premises. Mathi asked for my Government ID card and walked to a policeman on security and showed the card to him, and pointing his finger towards me, he said something. The policeman then came to me and said, "Sir, please come with me! I shall take you to the shrine." I just blindly followed him, and within 15 minutes, we were out of the temple. I thanked the policeman and walked back to the lodge. Our driver was there smoking his cigarette. We went to him and inquired, "Well, at what time shall we start tomorrow?" He said, "Sir, probably 11 AM in the morning. By the time you come back from the temple, it would be 10 AM or 10:30 AM, and maybe we can start then." I looked at him and said, "We finished visiting the temple, let's start at 6 AM." The driver was looking at us in utter disbelief. The next morning though we started at 6 AM, we had to wait till 7 AM for the gates to open. The local administration operates the traffic by putting gates and allowing vehicles in batches as the roads were highly dangerous. Once they opened the gates, we were the first to leave. On our way, we visited Joshi Mutt. This place holds importance for the fact that it is the winter seat of Lord Vishnu, whose idol is brought here from Badrinath shrine and ensconced during the cold season.

Continuing our drive, we were back at Rishikesh by evening. I asked the driver to take us to a bar for a drink and he said that Haridwar and Rishikesh are religious places so they don't sell liquor in these towns. However, he said he knew a place and drove us somewhere near Dehradun to a bar which was very close to a railway station.

We invited the driver for a drink and he joined us. He said that he had never in his life seen people like us who left in the morning and returned the very next day. He had packed clothes for four days and was now happy to be back in town to stay with his family. He said that the quick *darshans* we had in the temples were nothing but a miracle.

He told that people had to wait and stay for days here! Probably a miracle! Who knows! He later asked me an interesting question, "Don't you feel guilty that you are having a drink at the end of a religious trip?" The maverick that I am, I smiled and replied, "First, I do not consider drinking a vice, so there is no guilt. Next, I always have love for God, and I do not fear him; moreover, I am celebrating the fact that I could complete this trip without any hassles." He looked at me and said, "You are strange; you don't fit in this religious group." I smiled at him, acknowledging the fact and thought, "Maybe I don't, I don't know!"

There used to be a saying, "You don't choose to go to a Vishnu temple, It is Lord Vishnu who chooses who should come and when." This was true in our case. It was for our trip to Muktinath in Nepal. Mathi and I boarded a flight from Madras to Delhi and Delhi to Kathmandu, Nepal. By the time we reached Kathmandu, it was around 2 PM in the afternoon. After collecting our baggage, we came out to catch another flight to Pokhara. To our utter disbelief, all the flights were full. We didn't know how to proceed from there. It was then that we found a family who missed the Pokhara flight trying to hire a taxi. We offered to share and shortly joined them. It took us 8 hours to reach Pokhara. It was raining, and the roads were bumpy. Enjoying the Nepalese countryside along the journey, we arrived at Pokhara at around 10 PM in the night. We checked in at a hotel opposite the airport so that it would be easy to commute.

After a good sleep, we got up quite early and went to the airport to buy tickets for our flight to Jomsom, where there was another shock waiting for us. The staff said that they were not sure if the flights would fly as the weather was not conducive. The planes that fly to Jomsom are small aircrafts and they operate only when the skies are clear. They leave Pokhara early at around 6 AM in the morning and return by 10 AM. After ten, no flights operate as there would be strong gales in Jomsom. When we were at the airport, it was cloudy, and it appeared that no flights would take the risk of flying. Getting confirmation from the airline staff, we left for our hotel to go back to sleep. While we were there at the hotel, we heard the sound of aircraft flying. We rushed back to the airport and asked the airline staff, and they said, "Once you left, the sky cleared and our flights left!" I felt that maybe it was not destiny's wish for us to go to Muktinath this time. We went back and booked our tickets to Kathmandu, stayed there for two days, and visited the Pashupatinath Shiva Temple and other Buddhist monasteries, before returning home.

We again tried to visit the temple after a month. This time the Lord did show mercy on us. I contacted an agent in Kathmandu to help us with all the logistics and also did a lot of research regarding the weather conditions. This time, things went as per plan, and we reached Pokhara without any problems en route. The weather was excellent and the flight took off on time. The twenty minutes' travel was a rough ride with the airplane drifting and dipping at times. Once we reached Jomsom, we left our baggage at the local lodge and hired a van for a certain distance up to a stream. Once we crossed the stream, we rented a motorcycle to take us further. The last leg would be a walk for a kilometer or so. It was an all-inclusive journey; but for swimming, we did everything. We walked, drove, and flew. An interesting fact about the Gandaki river that passes near Muktinath is that, in the river bed, there are fossilised shell stones known as *Salagrama*. Devotees worship this natural stone as an iconic representation of Lord Vishnu. The local kids would dive and get us those stones for a little money.

The temple at Muktinath is one of the world's highest temples and is sacred for both the Buddhists and Hindus. The outer courtyard has a structure composed of 108 bull faces out of which water flows, probably signifying the water from the tanks of the 108 *Divya Desam* temples. After we visited the temple, we returned to the lodge at Jomsom. There I happened to meet a group of people from Tamil Nadu, led by an ascetic. I asked the group about the ascetic and they told me that he was Shri Velukudi Krishnan, a famous person in *Vaishnava* discourses. At that time, I knew nothing about him, but later in the years to come, I would become an ardent listener of his speeches. The people who had accompanied Shri Velukudi Krishnan were all *vaishnavites* and I could sense a subjective feeling in them. They were reluctant to talk to us and also looked down upon us. My friend was wearing a shirt which had *"Om Ganapati"* written all over. I could see a few commenting on the shirt and ridiculing - the reason being that Ganapati isn't a part of *Vaishnavism* but *Shaivism*. This hypocrisy and egotism is what one has to shed if one is for *sharanaagati* or surrender. Thanks to those people who taught me this concept through their unjust actions.

Many exciting incidents came to pass on these journeys. As a part of the *Divya Desam* tour, I had visited the Kal Azhagar Koil temple near Madurai. I had earlier seen the temple before I had any knowledge about the *Divya Desams.* This time when I entered the temple, there was a big white cloth covering the entrance to the *sanctum sanctorum.* There were no lights and none were allowed near the door. The idols were in a hall in front of the *sanctum sanctorum.* All prayers and rituals were happening there. The room was bright with lights while the *sanctum sanctorum* was dark. I asked the priest why they had covered the entrance and were not allowing people to go inside. He replied that for six months in a year, a herbal mixture called *"Taila Kaapu"* was applied to the main deity. *Taila Kaapu* means "armour of medicinal oils." These medicinal oils preserve the idols from any accidental damages that could potentially occur during the performance of rituals. After a certain period, they would remove it by pouring water with a herbal mixture. This water, which flows through the idol, is believed to have medicinal value for the devotees. I felt sad that having come to the temple, I couldn't get to worship the main deity. I requested the priest telling him that I was on a tour of 108 *Divya Desam,* and I would like to pray at the *sanctum sanctorum.* The priest said he couldn't remove the cloth, but instead, he would allow me to go up to the entrance where I could pray standing before the white fabric.

Thanking him for his permission, I entered the dark room, and when I came near the white cloth at the entrance to the *sanctum sanctorum,* the electric power went off. The whole temple was shrouded in darkness and at that made the *sanctum sanctorum* brighter. I could see the head of the deity above and the feet below the cloth. It was a goosebumps-inducing moment for me. I became very emotional; I prayed and gave my thanks for the divine *darshan* and slowly walked back. Once I came out of the room, the lights came on, and again the *sanctum sanctorum* went into darkness. I went to the priest and thanked him for his permission and narrated my experience. He said that it was a miracle and that I was blessed. It was for me that the power went off so that I could have the vision of the Lord. I once again thanked him and came out with contentment and satisfaction. Well, was that a miracle or just a coincidence? My rational mind asks.

Another spell-binding incident happened when Mathi and I were in Naimisaranyam, a *Divya Desam*, searching for the main temple. Naimisaranyam, or Neemsar, is a place around 80 km from Lucknow, a town in North India. We were aware that Naimisaranyam is a forest area where Lord Narayana resides in the entire flora, but we were looking for a temple as such. We were in that small forest area for nearly an hour searching for a temple, any temple. We lost hope and we were about to return when we found a priest walking towards us and enquiring after us in Tamil. Imagine someone in North India, where they speak only Hindi and not any other language, directly coming and talking to me in Tamil without knowing anything about me. Wasn't that a surprise?

I was pleased to see the priest and I told him about the purpose of our visit and our search for a temple to pay our obeisance. The priest then told us, "Naimisaranyam is a place where the Lord resides in the form of trees and shrubs." I asked him, "Well, Sir, then where do I pray, which tree should I bow to?" He immediately showed a tree next to him and said, "Pray to this one. Narayana is here in it." I was amazed to see an image of *Sricharanam* or *namam* painted on the tree. *Sricharanam* or *namam* is a religious symbol or mark worn on the foreheads by the followers of *Sri Vaishnavism,* which is in the form of Y or U in white with a red line in the middle. The Y or U represents the Lord and the red line, his consort. I stood there, prayed, and thanked them for the opportunity of visiting the place. It would have been just a minute or so, but when I turned to thank the priest, he was not there! I was stunned as there were no buildings around where he could have gone. I asked Mathi if he had seen him; he, too, was astonished to see the priest disappear. Was that a miracle or just a coincidence?

My journeys were mainly spiritual. I could never fit myself into any dogmas and always had trouble accepting the rules if they didn't make sense to me. They used to say that the *Divya Desam* tour should start from the Sri Rangam temple and end with the Thiruvengadam temple. I never followed that. I started as per my convenience and went on where my heart took me. They say that one should first take a dip in the holy lake and then visit the temple and one must spend a night in the town. I never did that. I do not find fault with the procedure, but I did things according to my time constraints. Seeing my interest in *Vaishnavism,* many had asked me why not get initiated into *Vaishnavism.* I told them, "To get initiated is building a wall around oneself, and one must strictly follow the rules and principles. I was not ready for that. I have trouble adhering to strict rules. Getting initiated and not following is nothing but showing disrespect, which I wouldn't do!" Some tell me not to eat non-vegetarian food on Saturdays as it is the day for Lord Vishnu. I find it a bit difficult to accept that. Why not other days? Does God specifically stay on Saturdays and not on other days? I think those people have a conflict within themselves. On one hand, love for their favourite meat and on the other, fear of God. Maybe to balance, they strike a compromise - one day for God and the other days for them. For me, there is God and Godliness everywhere, and it was always loving and not fearing.

"Sir, your Hindu non-vegetarian rice meal!" said the air hostess, handing over the food tray. I looked at her bemused. Was she listening to my thoughts?

VI

I opened up my plate and started to devour the contents. The food was tasty though it was in a small quantity. The ladies beside me were busy eating and conversing among themselves in Russian. After finishing my meal, carefully raising my tray, I got up, walked to the pantry, and placed it for the crew to clear. I was seated most of the time and I felt the need to stretch myself to relieve my cramped muscles. I gently walked, dodging the crew serving food, and reached the end of the aircraft. There were already a few people there. I smiled at the group and found a corner next to the toilet, stood there, folding and stretching my arms and legs. A young Indian guy, probably in his early 30s, came and stood next to me. Smiling at me, he asked, "Hi! Are you waiting for the restroom?" I replied in the negative. He then asked, "Where are you flying to?" I said, "To Chennai."

There was a surprise in his tone of reply and he said, "I am from Bangalore but my roots lie in Chennai." "Oh! That's nice to hear," I said, smiling ⁝m. "So I guess you work in the United States? ᐧᐣrk for the IT industry?" he asked.

ᐧᐧt work in the US. I work for the ᐧ in India." As expected, his ᐧ that's great! You guys are lucky!" and he went on with the obvious, "Well bro, I am carrying three bottles with me, can I sneak through the customs? Will they allow me?" I said, "Boss, I guess you are allowed to take only two, and for the third, you have to pay duty. Well, you better go to the customs counter and declare. They would surely guide you." Before he could go further on the subject, I quipped, "So you are the lucky one working in the US!" He frowned and said, "What is so great about it? I work for an IT company in Dallas. Those golden days are gone. I don't know when they will send me back. Too much uncertainty! Getting a permanent residency status is just a dream these days. I would be delighted to get back home rather than take this stress." There was sadness in his voice.

I got curious listening to him. Right from childhood, it was my dream to set foot in the US. When I was around 12 years of age, I remember reading the book, *Uncle Tom's Cabin* by Harriet Beecher Stowe which was part of our English subject curriculum. Though the novel was about anti-slavery, I visualised the natural beauty of the country through the words of the book. Apart from that, the works of Ayn Rand further nurtured my love for the US. I still remember her quote about America. "I can say—not as a patriotic bromide, but with full knowledge of the necessary metaphysical, epistemological, ethical, political and esthetic roots—that the United States of America is the greatest, the noblest and, in its original founding principles, the only moral country in the history of the world." This is from her book *Philosophy: Who Needs It*. Well, I never had the required peer group who could guide me, nor was my family financially sound to send me for higher education. It just remained a dream. Perhaps one day!

After I finished my tour of South East Asia, I decided to take up a trip to China. I approached a travel agent to process my visa. I had known this agent for quite some time, and when he flipped my passport, he said, "Sir, you have been to many countries. Why don't you apply for a US visa instead of China?" I said, "No, brother, I am scared. I know that once they reject your visa, it is tough to get it again. I don't want to take a chance." He retorted, "Unless you take a chance, how will you know whether you will get it or not?" He persuaded me to apply and said that he would take care of the process. With much reluctance, I paid the visa fees and was waiting for my allotted interview date. At the time of the visa interview, I dressed up formally, making myself look presentable. I was early at the embassy office and after mandatory security checks, they made me go to a hall with a token number and wait.

Waiting for my turn, I was observing the people go up the counter where some ended up arguing and some crying, and a few walked away happily. I was calculating the probability and it always seemed bleak for me. As they announced my turn, I could feel my heart come up my throat and my hands were starting to shiver. I walked up to the counter and handed my passport to an American lady who was seated there. I was worried about the fear of rejection. Had I not applied, I could always justify that since I never asked, so I never went to the US but I could go any time. But if rejected, I may not go at all! I took a few deep breaths and was ready.

The lady flipped through the pages and asked me, "Sir, why do you want to visit the US?"

I said, "Ma'am, I have a cousin who lives in Guam. I am planning to visit him." I handed over the invitation letter given by him.

She then asked, "Where do you work?" I said, "I work for the Government" and showed my papers.

She went through the pages of the passport and stopped at a page. She then asked, "Why did you go to Cambodia?"

"I love to travel, ma'am. I went backpacking."

"Your visa is approved. You will get your passport in a few days. You may leave." she said, keeping my passport with her.

I went blank. Did she just say that my visa was approved? Is this all true? I could not believe myself. It took a few seconds to come back to my senses. I walked out silently with all the joy and happiness contained in me ready to explode. The road opposite the embassy was a quiet avenue. I walked up there and all of a sudden, I started jumping with joy! YESSSS! My visa to the US has been approved!

The restroom door opened and my Chennai friend quickly entered before someone else could occupy it.

VII

Though my visa was approved, I did not immediately take up a tour of the US. There were some financial constraints and I had to wait for a year to embark on my journey. In the meanwhile, I started my planning. There was this vague thought which was there on my mind – "Why not plan something big?" I pondered upon the idea and then jotted down a mega travel plan. A travel plan spread over two months.

It was in late October that I took off on a British Airways flight to the US. After a tedious flight of 22 hours, I landed at Ronald Reagan International Airport, Washington. As a kid, I was in awe of everything I saw. I was expecting everything to be in Eastman colour like in the Hollywood movies. Stepping out of the aircraft, I walked to the immigration and my first interaction was very pleasant. The officer at the counter asked about my visit and my profession. When I said that I work for the Indian Customs, there was a genuine cheerfulness in inviting me. He spoke to me for quite some time, enquiring about my duties, and comparing it with his. He welcomed me to the US with a stamp on my passport. I felt a sense of joy and pride in my profession. It was 7 PM in the evening by the time I collected my bags and walked out of the airport. The weather was chilly and I slipped on my jacket. Whenever the Pope visits a country, he would get down and kiss the land. Likewise, I just sat on the road and felt the ground with my bare hands. My taxi had arrived by then and I was off to the Hilton hotel at Alexandria. I stayed put in the hotel for a day trying to get over my jet lag and the following day started my trip. I had booked a guided bus tour to cover a part of the east coast - this was not my style of travelling; but to cover places in a short period, this was the only option.

Our trip started with a visit to the Capitol Hill, Lincoln Memorial, the Obelisk, a look at the White House from a distance, and ended with a cruise in the Potomac River. From there, we took off to New Jersey to retire for the night. The tourists on our tour bus were mostly from China, and the only non-Chinese were me, two Australian ladies, and a Colombian couple. It was fun for us on the whole trip. Being a minority in the bus which we fondly called it as "The Manchurian Express", we five became a closed knit group. We would eat and visit places together. On the bus, I was seated next to an old Chinese woman. She kept on talking to me in Mandarin, not bothered about the fact that I couldn't understand a word. I tried to explain to her in English that I don't speak Mandarin, but she didn't give a damn so I nodded my head and smiled at times giving her the feeling that I understood her. At times she would ask a question and look at me for an answer. I wouldn't have a clue that it was a question, and as usual, I would just smile, and she would continue with her blather.

From New Jersey, the bus took us directly to Buffalo, where we had a spectacular view of the Niagara Falls. It was icy cold and I was shivering despite my winter clothing. By evening there were colourful lights focused on the falls, and the waters kept changing their mood with the change of colours. The colossal falls with the loud sound was once again a majestic manifestation of nature displaying its behemothic power. The evening passed pleasantly with the Australian ladies sharing memories of travel over drinks. It was with much satisfaction and a sense of fulfillment that I retired to bed.

We had to get up very early next day and board the bus which would take us to Boston. But for the cruise, we didn't explore much of Boston. The one saving factor was the famous Boston lobster dinner we had. From Boston, we headed to Harvard, MIT, and finally to our destination in New York. New York is that one place I can never forget. I stayed in Manhattan for two days and my evenings included a stroll from Times Square, a place with positive vibrations, to the Grand Railway Station, a backdrop in many Hollywood movies. The glorious architecture takes you 100 years back in time. A cruise to Ellis Island and the Statue of Liberty, a walk on Wall Street, and then to the World Trade Center Memorial occupied my last day there.

Taking the bus trip was a mistake for many reasons. Being a solo traveller, I would have gone on my own and at my own pace and leisure. I felt like I was rushed to various places in a short span of time. We would get to a hotel and retire at 11 PM in the night and again we should be ready by 5

AM in the lobby. The tour guide was like our master and we were his obedient lackeys. I always had the feeling that I was at gunpoint throughout the trip. Well, it had its greener side too. I ended up making a lot of friends, some of whom are still in contact with me. I also learned some discipline and manners on the bus. Usually, when the bus stops and we have to get down, I always rush to the front, trying to get down first. I did the same that day, and Sue, the Australian lady rebuked me, "Why do you rush? You know everyone has to get down. A minute wait wouldn't cost much, will it?" I saw how disciplined and well behaved the people were on the bus. None stood up, and people got down row-wise. I realised my mistake and waited my turn. It was a lesson learned on the trip. Thanks to my friend Sue! The next day I took a flight and flew to Miami.

In contrast with the cities up north, Miami had pleasant weather. I had booked a hostel closer to South beach. The hostel was hosting a barbeque night the evening I landed. The introvert that I am, I picked up a bottle of beer and sat in a dark corner with a hot dog to eat. A couple of beers down my throat, I was there in the centre laughing and chatting with a group of friends from Brazil, Portugal, and Monaco. The next morning the Brazilian friend and I started early. The Brazilian could speak only Portuguese, his mother tongue, and no other languages. I had to converse with him in my broken Spanish, and to date, I never know how we got along together. Neither of us knew the language the other was speaking. But still, we were conversing and went on a cruise around Miami, and then on our return, we visited the Cuban colony. After a nap and dinner, I joined my Portuguese friend and bar-hopped the entire night. By the time we reached the hostel, we were pitch drunk.

The next day I spent on the beach. It was like a colourful picture with the light blue sky merging with the dark blue sea and finishing off with a white beach. The beautiful people added a rainbow of colours to the image. Lying down under a shade, with the pleasant breeze whizzing past, it was one of the best relaxing moments I experienced. Next to me was a young lady sitting on a long chair. She was with a group and it was just a matter of time before we started conversing. She was a German and was on vacation to Miami with her office mates. After chatting for an hour or so, we decided to meet at a local bar in the evening. It was a famous night club that played Latin music. She had come with her group and me with my Portuguese friend. We started with beers and ended up dancing till late into the night. As though something possessed me, I turned profligate that night and was spending money buying rounds for the whole group. When I left for my hostel early the next morning, I realised that there was just a paltry amount left in my wallet. I had a month and a half of travelling left, and here I was, with only a few dollars in hand.

I was worried about my expenditure and decided to stay thrifty all through my journey. A saving factor was that I had paid for all my hostels and flights for the trip, just that I didn't have the spare money for my extravagances. Like a saviour from the heavens, my friend Vinod called me to enquire about my trips. When I narrated my experience the previous night to him, without any hesitation, he deposited sufficient money in my account without me even asking for it. He told me that experience is an experience – good or bad and I should just enjoy it. He asked me to follow my heart and not my mind. With money in hand and encouragement from him, I was ready for my onward journey to Brazil to start my tour of the South American continent.

After a month's travel, I returned to the US. My port of entry was Houston. While waiting for my turn at immigration, I happened to meet an Indian family. As there was a long line ahead of me, I started a conversation with them. He introduced himself as Saravanan, and with him were his wife and their ten year old daughter. While we were talking, the daughter and her mother were engaged in their own conversation. Their conversation was in English. I interrupted them and said, "Sorry to be nosy. Why don't you speak with your kid in Tamil? Can't she speak the language?" Her mother replied, "No, we try to speak, but she is comfortable in English." I said, "I am sorry to say this. It's good to be able to speak and understand English, but it would be even better to speak in her mother tongue. It would help her remain connected to her roots and ethnic identity." They quite understood and accepted their folly. We exchanged numbers and they invited me to their house in Los Angeles if I happened to pass by the city. I said that I would surely make it, bid them goodbye and took a flight to Las Vegas, where my sister and her husband were waiting for me.

My brother-in-law Segar is a travel lover who has travelled to more than a hundred countries! I always rely on him for tips and advice for my trips. On my arrival, I checked into the hotel they were in and what else – it's Vegas! We partied all night. I was never a gambling enthusiast, so I just went around the casinos while Segar tried his luck on the console machines. The sin city was too colourful and too vibrant for me to comprehend. I was probably more a person of nature. After spending a couple of days in Vegas, we drove to the huge Hoover Dam and from there to Chevron, where we rested in a motel and then continued the next morning to the Grand Canyon.

It was a beautiful drive to the Grand Canyon. Tall trees on both sides of the road and remnants of ice as a result of last night's snowfall made the scenic drive delightful. On reaching the destination, we parked our car and went to the reception centre for information. From there, we took a short walk to the visitor's point. As I stepped in, it was nothing short of a breathtaking view. The vast landscape was overwhelming. The whole range was painted in different layers of colours. The red colour, interspersed with blue, green and pink of the layers presented a colourful feast to the eyes. Nature keeps on surprising me with its different shades of beauty and I always wonder how much more there is in store for me. While I was indulging in the beauty of the Canyon, it started to snow, and we had to run back to our cars. The fall was so heavy that by the time we reached our car, it was covered in a blanket of snow. I took the keys and experienced my first drive through a snowfall.

Moving slowly and finding my way amidst the white mist, I successfully navigated the snowy terrain and parked in a pit stop for a hot chocolate. Segar took the wheels from there, and we drove to Barstow, where we rested for the night. Next day we drove to Anaheim and visited the Disney Land. From Anaheim, it was Los Angeles and from there to San Francisco.

San Francisco is another human-made beauty with the Golden Gates Bridge, Alcatraz Prison Island, and many more iconic landmarks. What attracted me the most was the Lombardy Street or the East-West Street, a steep road with many hairpin bends. There is a section also known as the most crooked street in the world. A view from the bottom end of the road makes the lane look like a long serpent slithering up.

With Segar and my sister leaving for Singapore, I was left alone for the next five days to roam around. I checked into a hostel in the Bay area, met a German there, and got talking. I was narrating my driving experience from Las Vegas to SFO when he asked me if I had taken the route number 1 from Los Angeles to San Francisco. I said no, and he immediately said, "Brother, you are missing something big! You should experience it." He didn't say a word further. I thought about it and immediately called Saravanan, whom I had met at Houston Airport and told him that I was coming to Los Angeles. He was more than happy to welcome me. I immediately booked a car from Dollar Cars - a car renting agency and started the next morning to Los Angeles. I took the highway route 101 and in seven hours I reached LA. Saravanan accommodated me at a friend's place for the night.

The next day, he arranged tickets to visit Universal Studios. It was a great experience visiting the

Studios. What I liked the most were the locations and sets, which had figured in some of the great Hollywood flicks. It was my first visit to any theme park and I instantly fell in love with it. After the visit to the studios, Saravanan was waiting for me to take me to Hollywood and Beverly Hills. He patiently showed me around, gave details of the places, and then he took me out for a drink. When we reached home, his wife was ready with some hot spicy Indian food, which I had been craving for many days. After a satisfying meal, he took me for a drive and loaded my car with enough gas for my trip back to SFO. He also booked a motel for my stay the following night at Gilroy as it would be too late by then. I stayed at his place for the night, and the next day I started my journey back to SFO; but this time I was on US route no. 1.

After crossing the bustling traffic of LA, I hit US route no. 1. It was a quiet road with not much traffic. It was a leisurely drive for me. Sipping an Americano, listening to the songs on the radio, driving with the window glass slightly down and feeling the chill air, I was mentally thanking the German for suggesting the route. A few miles down the road, I was overwhelmed to see the vast Pacific Ocean on my left and the green forest on my right. It is probably one of the best scenic drives in the world. There were stops in between where we could relax by the beach and see the seals resting alongside. On the way, I happened to cross an architectural marvel, the Bigsby Creek Bridge, situated on the Big Sur coast of California. It is the tallest and the highest single-span arch bridge in the world and also the most photographed bridges in California, especially for its aesthetic design. Enjoying every minute of the ride, I, at last, reached Gilroy at about 8 PM in the night. I picked some beers and food and checked into my room. That was the last night of my trip.

The next morning I had to reach SFO by 11 AM and was slated to catch the 4 PM flight to India. I was reliving the experience of the drive, and at one point, I started to sob. I was cursing my fate. Why hadn't I come and settled in the US like others? Why is God just showing me a glimpse of everything and letting it go? Much more than what Ayn Rand had to say, Nature had shown me what a spotless beauty it was. The words of Ayn Rand again rung in my mind, "Contradiction never exists in nature. If you find one, check your premise." Yes, what I had seen is beauty sans contradiction; it was prissiness in its purest form. This journey gave me the opportunity of meeting a beautiful human being, Saravanan, and I felt thankful for all the love and affection he had shown me. He was an example of how a good human being could be. This journey made me realise and feel the connection I had with nature and, by extension with God.

The next morning I left Gilroy and headed directly to SFO airport and dropped my car there, checked-in for my flight to India, and boarded with contentment.

"Sir, please return to your seat, the pilot has switched on the seat belt sign, sir!" the air hostess requested. I said, "Sure, ma'am, let me use the restroom before I go," and I stepped into the toilet. Once back to my seat, I saw the ladies in a deep sleep. I opened the window. It was so bright that I had to shut it back down. Wondering how many hours had passed, I felt for my watch, but it wasn't there.

VIII

While I was wondering where I could have dropped my watch, the air hostess came rushing towards my seat and said, "Sir, you forgot something!" I said, "I forgot?" "Yes, your watch in the restroom" "Oh! I was wondering where I'd lost it. Thank you so much." "You are welcome, sir." and she left, handing me my wristwatch. The crew dimmed the lights in the aircraft, I closed my eyes and began thinking about what else I had forgotten. It then struck me that I had forgotten the whole South and Central American trip which I took along with the US trip.

The idea of taking a mega trip was to cover both the continents in one go as it would be a financially prudent decision. The planning started a year before my travel. It included browsing the net and enriching my knowledge about the countries. As South and Central American countries are predominantly Spanish speaking, I realised that knowledge of the Spanish language would come in handy. So I enrolled in a Spanish learning institute. As a part of this preparation, I endeavoured to study the Latin cultures and realised that dance formed an integral part of their lives and that their favourite dance form was Salsa! My knowledge of Salsa was minimal -

limited in the sense that it was just a food topping and not feet tapping to a rhythm. Having decided to learn the dance form, I enrolled in a dance school.

Spanish and Salsa go hand in hand. The songs they danced to in Salsa are Spanish songs and listening to them helped me learn the language a bit faster. Learning Salsa opened up another gate of happiness in my life. It was quite an experience to fight my shyness. I went through all sorts of inconvenience in the course of learning. My dancing started slowly from just doing the basics and then improved by adding a few turns and moves. It being a partner-dance, I had varied experiences with different partners. Well, I have had the good, the bad, and the ugly experiences on the dance floor. I have been left on the dance floor by a girl in the middle of a dance. I have been refused for a dance by one girl for as many times as I have asked her. I also met a girl who came to my rescue when these things happened.

I had learned one important thing as far as dancing is concerned. For any learner of Salsa, the doom usually comes in the form of a beautiful woman who has just begun to learn to dance. When you dance with a woman who is new to Salsa and when you try some tricky moves, she would naturally be awestruck and would say that you are an excellent dancer; and therein spells doom for a growing dancer. It would get to your head and the learning process would come to a grinding halt. Probably I think this bug must have bitten most of them, as I have seen many who are still at the same level of dancing despite years of learning. The dance floor is one great place that segregates people by their character and actions. It is so awesome that one can check where he stands in the social circle. I can compare the dance floor to the sea. If one has strictly observed the sea, he can understand that the sea retains things that are good to it and washes the undesirable to the coast be it dead fish or debris - eventually, it all comes back to the shore. It is just a matter of time! The same way, the dance floor retains only the people who have come for dance and washes the rest to the fringes of the floor! That's the beauty! If you happen to dance on the floor, then it means the sea has accepted you as its treasure! What I learned from the dance floor is "dance is for the sake of dance" not for any motives, ulterior or superior!

Once confident that I could communicate in Spanish, I embarked on my mega journey. I went to the US, and after visiting parts of the East Coast, I took off from Miami to Rio de Janeiro in Brazil. The journey took around 12 hours, as I had to change flights to arrive at the destination. On arrival, I took a taxi to the Copacabana area and checked in at a hostel where I was given a bunker to rest. I was too tired from the journey and slept through the day. The next morning, I walked to a bakery or *padaria* as they say in Portuguese. I ordered bread, cheese, and coffee. Bread is known as *pao,* like in Bombay. I then learned that *pao* was a result of the Portuguese influence on the common language of Bombay. The city was once a Portuguese settlement but was later given as dowry to the British for the marriage of Prince Charles II with the Portuguese princess Catherine of Braganza.

After breakfast, I left with some friends from the hostel to see the favelas. Our visit was to the Rocinha hill, which houses the shanty slums called favelas. They are one large cluster with tightly bound dingy residences. Once you enter, it would be difficult to find a way out. Houses were built all over the hill and we could see bullet holes on the walls signifying their notoriety. Inside the favela, the residents looked at us with suspicion and we explained to them that we were tourists; it was then that there were friendly smiles all around.

From the Rocinha hill, we took a car and drove up to the Christ the Redeemer statue, which is one of the Seven Wonders of the World. Situated on top of the Corcovado Mountain, the colossal statue of Christ with his arms spread out seemed like the Lord reaching out to embrace and bless the city. Our next stop was Escadaria Selaron, or the steps of Lapa, where tiles from all over the world were brought in and glued on the 200 odd steps along with its adjoining walls, making it a beauty of its own. I searched for the tiles from India and took a photograph. Likewise, my friends from the hostel went in search of the tiles from their respective countries.

Our next stop was the Sugarloaf Mountain. It is a monolithic mountain resembling a sugarloaf facing the Atlantic Ocean. We could reach the mountain peak by a cable car or the *teleferico* as they call it in Brazil, and we got a breathtaking view of the city of Rio. We also sighted the famous Maracana stadium from there. On returning to the hostel, I passed my evening with a long walk from the famous Ipanema beach to the also equally famous

Copacabana beach. Ipanema is probably one of the best beaches I have ever seen. It was around November end and a pleasant time to visit Brazil as I could see a lot of tourists surfing, sunbathing, and socialising. It was nearing sunset as I walked across the Copacabana beach, which is in the shape of a crescent where a lot of people were enjoying the evening breeze. Adjacent to the beach was a neatly tiled pavement for the walkers. I walked for a while and when I realised I was tired, I walked across the road to find a bar and chill for the night.

Though Rio de Janeiro was the only city I had visited in Brazil, it had given me a feel of the Brazilian life. Brazilians are friendly people who do not hesitate to smile when they pass by a stranger. I have seen this in all the Latin American countries I visited. They have this beautiful habit of wishing strangers at the elevator or restaurants with *Bom Dia,* meaning good morning. It feels so lovely to be welcomed. I have this delightful incident to narrate which tells a lot about the South Americans in general and Brazilians in particular. My next destination was Lima, Peru. My flight was a red-eye, at 5 AM in the morning. I left my hostel at around 1 AM. I was there at the airport by 2 AM, and when I reached the departure counter, there was not a single soul. Probably I was too early. I waited there at the desk for an hour and a half and I could see people coming and standing at different places, not forming a line. Feeling sleepy, I went to a nearby cafeteria for some hot coffee. By the time I finished my coffee and returned to the counter, there was a long line of people waiting to check-in. I cursed myself for leaving the desk and I sauntered to the end of the line. It was then people from the front called me and said, "Sir, please come and stand here. You were the first to arrive!" It was a beautiful, heartwarming experience to witness the courteousness of the people. The world would surely be a beautiful place if everyone had this honesty and politeness.

My next destination was Lima, Peru. Lima was just a stopover to Cuzco, a town from where you go to Machu Picchu, another one of the Seven Wonders of the World. Arriving at Lima, I took a taxi to the central part of the City where I had booked my accommodation. As usual, the first day was devoted to relaxing and sleeping. I spent the next day exploring the cuisine of Peru. Peru is renowned for being the food capital of the Latin lands. I scouted the best restaurants in the city and decided to walk so that I could have a better experience of the town and, in the process, build up my appetite. Being in Lima, one can never miss *ceviche.* It is a dish made of squids, raw fish, and shrimps soaked in lime. It has a tangy taste with a tinge of spice. I also tried the *apanado de alpaca,* a dish made from the meat of Alpaca (an animal species of the South American Camelid) with rice, potatoes, and some green salad. Both the dishes were a feast for the palate. I rounded off the meal with a hot black coffee.

The next day, I took a bus to Cuzco, a town in Peru. The journey would be for 22 hours and the bus had all the amenities like restrooms, comfortable seats. They also served food and coffee at intervals. I preferred to take the bus as it would give me a glimpse of the Peruvian countryside. As usual, the kid that I am, I took a window seat and was glued to it all through the journey. The trip was meandering and at times felt like we were climbing at a leisurely pace, catching up with the altitude. One could feel the altitude difference with Lima, a height of around 500 ft above sea level, and Cuzco with an elevation of about 11,000 ft. Initially, it was interesting to view the countryside, but later, boredom crept in, and I began counting the minutes to get off the bus and have a proper sleep in a real bed.

Getting down in Cuzco, after a trying 22 hour bus ride, the first thing I felt was breathlessness. At 11,000 ft, it is but a common phenomenon. At the hotel, the staff gave me a glass of hot water with crushed cacao leaves. They say it is a local remedy for breathlessness. I felt much better after drinking it. There were also oxygen cylinders lined up for tourists with graver problems. After resting for the day, I woke up fresh the next morning and started early to check the local sites. My first stop was the Plaza de Armas, the main city square of Cuzco. It was a vibrant and busy market space with shops and eateries. With the cobbled pavements and a majestic fountain at the centre, it gave a feel of being transported to the colonial period. A few minutes from there, I visited the temple of the Gods of the Incas. They were just stone monuments and nothing else. The gold which once adorned these temples has now disappeared. Courtesy the Spanish conquests, the Incas were stripped of their wealth.

From there, I visited a Church called the *Señor de Los Temblores,* or the Lord of Earthquake. The church, which dates back to the 16th century, houses an idol of the crucifixion of Jesus Christ which had turned black from centuries of exposure to smoke, dust, soot, and various other vagaries of nature. There was gold all the way covering the walls and doors, probably the Inca Gold. Another charming thing that I noticed was the painting of the *Last Supper*. It was an Incanised version of Da Vinci's classic. In this painting, we find the meat of a guinea pig placed on the table in front of Christ. It was a delicacy for the Incas, and they delighted in savouring it on all important occasions. The inclusion of native food in the *Last Supper* is a perfect example of Incanisation of Christianity and a classic anthropological example of how one culture fuses with another. After a beautiful city tour, I winded up my day at the local bar tasting the famous Peruvian drink *Pisco Sour* and was back in my hotel as I had to get ready for an early trip to Machu Picchu the following day.

I started off early to the railway station at Poroy in Cuzco to catch a train to Agua Calientes, the last stop from where I had to take a bus to Machu Picchu. The train ride was quite a beautiful and a memorable trip. Through the large panoramic windows and the glass ceiling, I could see the snow-clad peaks and have a 360 degree view of scenic beauty. The crew of the train served food and coffee at regular intervals, and there was a fashion show too to enthrall us. The 3 hour ride passed away quickly.

On reaching Agua Calientes, I took a bus to Machu Picchu, and within 40 minutes, I was there at the Reception centre. I purchased my ticket and promptly made friends with a Russian couple, an American, and a Chinese. We went as a group exploring the human-made wonder. A symbol of the Incan empire, Machu Picchu is known for its architectural excellence where they built dry stone walls without the use of mortar. Consisting of houses, temples, baths, and other structures, it is one of the few cities of the Inca Civilisation which escaped the onslaught of Spanish Conquests because of its hidden location and by being invisible from low land. Viewed from a high vantage point, it gives a picture of how Mother Nature allows a civilisation to nourish and grow in her lap when you obey and respect her.

Winding my trip at Machu Picchu, I flew from Cuzco to Lima and then to Bogota, Colombia, and onward to Cucuta. Cucuta is a border town that lies near the frontier of Venezuela. While I was learning Spanish, I had enrolled myself in an online site where I could meet people who would teach and converse with me in Spanish, and I, in turn, would guide and chat in English. In the process, I made a lot of Latin friends. One such friend was Maria Isabel, a sweet looking lady who was waiting at the airport to receive me. On landing at Cucuta, she took me to her place, and that was my first experience of being with a Latin family. I got first-hand exposure to Latin culture. I met her family and relatives and they hosted a barbeque night for me. It was an enjoyable experience to be with a Latino family, who never cared about the next day and embraced the present to the fullest. The next day she took me for a drive to a small town on a hill called Chinacota. It was a beautiful, small, laid-back town with a church in the centre and a town square adjacent to it. We spent a few hours there and drove down to the border town to make our purchases for our travel to Venezuela. Isabel bought rolls and rolls of toilet paper and I wondered why.

The next day we started our journey to Merida, Venezuela, to meet another friend, Oriana Montufar. We crossed the border and entered the small town of San Antonio on the Venezuelan side and loaded our car with gasoline. I was shocked to learn that gas, or petrol as we call it back home in India, was more or less free. We paid just a few cents for a full tank! Yes, the country was rich in oil resources. From San Antonio we drove down to a bigger town called San Christobal. We stayed for the night at Isabel's friend's place. It was a memorable night with the family who was very curious to learn about India; they seemed to be in awe, enthralled especially with the Indian Gods and the elephant-headed Ganesha in particular. We partied and danced late into the wee hours.

The next afternoon we drove to Merida, and by the time we reached, it was 5PM in the evening. As we entered the city, we could see lines and lines of people waiting outside mostly empty supermarkets. It was probably a year after the death of Hugo Chavez, the president of Venezuela. The country had slipped quickly into an economic disorder. Primary and bare necessities were difficult to get. Once a relatively wealthy country with abundant natural resources, it has now joined the ranks of the poorest countries just because of wrong economic policies. Years of Socialist policies with free handouts to the people had pushed the country into a deep financial turmoil. When we went to meet Oriana, I gifted her an ethnic Indian handbag, and she thanked me for it. When Isabel gave the rolls of toilet paper she had bought from Colombia, immediately, the whole family joined in hugging and thanking her for being so thoughtful. It was quite an emotional moment. A roll of toilet paper now was worth more than anything else for the once-wealthy nation!

The next few days, we went sightseeing in and around Merida. The one not-to-be-missed place is the Mountain of Dreams or *La Montana De Los Suenos*. It is a theme park that houses an automobile museum displaying a collection of vintage cars, a cinema studio with different sets and locations, and many other interesting artefacts. The other one is the Antiers of Venezuela. The theme of this park is the Venezuela of the 1920s. Apart from having a museum of antiquities, it has different segments named after the various states of the country, each portraying its unique culture and tradition. In this theme park, the shows demonstrated Venezuelan traditions with refreshing humour. From Merida, back to Cucuta, and again here, I had the unique experience of attending a *Quinceañera* celebration of the daughter of one of Isabel's friends. It was a celebration of a girl's 15th birthday to mark her passage from girlhood to womanhood. The party began with the birthday girl dressed in a beautiful gown and a tiara cutting the birthday cake, followed by a waltz dance with the father of the girl, and then everyone gets to dance with her. Food, drinks, and dancing were always at the backdrop in Latin celebrations. I got my chance to swing my legs to the tune of the music with the locals and it was a night of fun and frolic.

Bidding bye to my friend Isabel, it was time to explore Colombia. At Bogota, I had my other online friend Oscar waiting for me. Bogota, being at a high altitude, was on the chilly side. I stayed in a local hostel and the next day Oscar took the responsibility of acting as a tour guide to show me the city from Mount Monserrate to the Oro Gold Museum. Mount Monserrate is a mountain over 10,000 ft and dominates the centre of Bogota. Atop there is a Catholic shrine which we visited by a cable car. The Oro Museum, one of the most visited tourist attractions, houses the most extensive collection of artefacts of gold and other precious stones and metals.

A couple of more days in Bogota and we flew off to Cali, the Salsa Capital of the World. Oscar and his girlfriend accompanied me to the city. Cali is a city with many clubs in its suburb. My only reason for visiting Cali was to try my dancing skills in the Mecca of Salsa! On the day of arrival, we spent the time visiting a scenic hilltop adorned by the statue of Jesus Christ called Cristo Rey, probably, Colombia's answer to Brazil's Christ the Redeemer. We spent time enjoying the scenic view from the hilltop before we got back to get ready for our night of dancing and revelry. We started club-hopping, drinking a few beers in each club, and only late in the night did the crowd begin to pour in. We got to a decent club and bought a bottle of Ron, the local Colombian rum, and started to party. As usual I was shy in the beginning, but as time passed by and when Ron began its work, I was on my toes displaying my professional dancing skills to the surprise of my Colombian friends. They could never believe that an Indian could dance Salsa so well. It was 4 AM in the morning when we left the club. It was a memorable night. I broke out of my shell and danced to my heart's content. Usually, I have this feeling of worrying what the other person would think of me, would he make fun of me, was my dance good enough – all these pessimistic questions were put to rest that night. None in the club were interested in me; they were busy enjoying themselves, and I was enjoying the display of my recently acquired skill. To quote Vicki Baum, the Austrian writer, "There are shortcuts to happiness, and dancing was one of them". Yes, I lived the shortcut that night!

Oscar and his friend left for Bogota after an emotional parting and I headed to Medellin – the City of Eternal Springs. The second largest city in Colombia had a pleasant weather. I didn't visit the typical tourist attractions; instead, I opted to mingle with the common public. I took up the local metro and the *teleferico,* a cable car service, and travelled with the locals. The cable car was a unique transport system to access the neighbourhood or the Barrios, which lay on the hills and are otherwise rather inaccessible. It was an experience in itself; travelling in a box and mingling with the local crowd who hop in and hop off at stops. After spending the next two days traversing the city, I left for Panama. At the airport, I couldn't resist ordering Colombian food - it became one of my favourite Latin American cuisines. I picked up an *Arroz Frito con Pescado* and capped the meal with a hot cup of the world-famous Colombian coffee. I could sense the aroma of fresh coffee still lingering and the smell was so strong that it woke me up from my thoughts to behold the crew serving hot coffee. The temptation was too good to resist - I asked for a hot coffee, and sipping it, I slipped comfortably back into my thoughts.

IX

My journey now took me to Central America.
Panama is on the isthmus connecting South
America with Central America. It was Panama City
where I landed and, as usual, accommodated
myself in a local hostel in the city centre. Panama
is a beautiful city with a lovely beach lined with
towering sky rise buildings. The twisted tower is
one that inspired awe in me; I was amazed by the
imagination of the human mind. The majesty of
these high sky rise towers was dwarfed only by the
exquisite beauty of the colonial structures that
dotted the city. On one of the evenings, I took a
stroll along the beach, immersed in the mix of
natural beauty on one side and the human-made
architectural splendour on the other. Enjoying the
view, I walked till dark, and it was then that I
realised I had walked four kilometers. I took a turn
and walked back the 4 kilometers to my hostel,
this time being careful not to be mugged by some
delinquents. The next day, I hired a taxi to see the
splendour of the colonial architecture and to also
visit the famous Panama Canal.

Back in the hostel lobby, there was a discussion
on the bioluminescent bay in Puerto Rico among
the travellers. I was there listening to their
conversations eagerly. The travellers were sharing

their experiences. It was then that I got to know that bioluminescence is the emission of light by marine organisms and they are in abundance in Puerto Rico. That was enough for a nature lover like me. I immediately scrambled my itinerary and rescheduled my trip to include Puerto Rico by sacrificing a few days, which I otherwise would have been spending at the San Blas archipelago, Panama.

San Juan, the capital of Puerto Rico, is another lovely city on the Atlantic coast. My stay was very close to the sea near Castillo de San Cristobal, a colossal fort. As my purpose was to see the bioluminescent bay, I was quick to book a tour that same night. I did learn that there are only a few sites left which could boast of bioluminescence, and the Mosquito Bay in Fajardo is one of them. Thanks to civilisation, this luminescence is fast dwindling and is on its way to extinction. With my expectation and excitement building up, I waited for my pickup to arrive. It arrived at 8 PM and took me to Fajardo, which was an hour's drive, and from there, I, along with a few tourists, took off in a small oar boat. It was pitch dark and we rowed into the swamps. I had my hands on the oar; after a few minutes of rowing, we saw a flash of glow in the dark waters. Once I touched the waters, there was this neon blue-green glow around my hands. It was as though we were in the midst of heavenly waters. Once again, we became kids splashing our hands in the waters and seeing the light glow. It was indeed another spectacle of this beautiful world. Mother Nature, through these wonders, flashes her immenseness, always surprises me, and reminds me of the romantic relationship I share with her.

Then there was this incident that occurred in San Juan, and whenever I think of it, I can't stop my laughter. Walking the cobbled streets around the tourist sites, I found a souvenir shop and went inside to buy something. The owner was a Chinese who was very friendly and I had a good chat with him. He was happy to know that I was from India and was very interested in my travels. After our chatting came to a logical end, I told him that I would like to buy something which has Puerto Rico printed on it, and he showed me a section where there were a lot of items on display. I went and picked up a beautiful T-shirt that had the Puerto Rico map printed on it. I took it to the counter and told the guy that I would take this. He looked at the T - shirt then looked at me and said, "Are you sure?" I said, "Yes, I am sure!" He replied, "Think again because once you pay, you cannot exchange!" I was confused. I said, "Why will I exchange? I already tried and it fits me." He said, "Ok, then you pay me first, and then I shall tell you why." Puzzled by what he was saying, I paid for the T-shirt and bought it. He then said, "Well, now look at it," and he flipped the tag at the collar of the T-shirt and asked me to read it. It had a print that said, "Made in India." I broke into a riotous laugh when he said, "You came all the way from India to buy an Indian T-shirt!"

San Jose, Costa Rica, was my next destination. This country is very close to my heart for its abundant natural beauty. Having coastlines with both the Caribbean Sea and the Pacific Ocean, it is a country with different types of rainforests. This time, I checked in at a hotel and not a hostel, just to pamper myself with some luxurious solitude. It was here that I met an American from Dallas,

USA, and we became good friends just over a conversation at the hotel's bar. We both ventured out the next day to the thick rain forest area for a zip line and rappelling adventure. The forest was too dense and thick and reminded me of the rainforests of Malaysia.

We had our helmets and other protective gear; sheer adrenaline rush kicked in as we zipped through the forest and brooks. The zip line ended with rappelling which made my heart leap to my throat. The following day we went to the Poas Volcano and National Park. There were a lot of tourists as it was one of the most visited tourist spots, but unfortunately, none could see the crater due to bad weather. However, we could smell the occasional whiff of sulphur emitting out of the volcano. We waited for the clouds to clear but in vain. We later walked a trail into the national park. It was a vast and well-maintained park with a plethora of flora and fauna. It was one of the best experiences I ever had, treading carefully on the slippery path with huge waterfalls on a side, spraying chill waters on us. Should I get another chance, Costa Rica would surely be on the itinerary.

Next on the list was Guatemala City, Guatemala. This time I chose a homestay at an old lady's quarters. This lady was kind enough to arrange a taxi for me to visit Antigua – an ancient colonial city built by the Spanish and surrounded by volcanoes. Though the distance was around 30 kilometers, it took us an hour to reach there. On the way, I asked the driver to stop at some restaurant for breakfast. He took me to a decent place. When I entered, the doorman smiled at me and said, *"Buenos Días, Señor!"* meaning *Good morning, Sir.* I, as usual, nodded my head and walked inside. The driver looked bewildered. He asked me, "Sir, why didn't you respond to the doorman?" I said, "Yes, I did. I nodded my head in gesture." He said, "No, Sir! It is an insult when you don't respond to someone who says, *"Buenos Dias".* You don't nod your head. You are not his boss. He is only serving you." The driver was straightforward. I then understood the equality of men and the dignity of labour in the country. I realised my folly, and I kept quiet and had my breakfast. On my way out, I stopped at the doorman, tipped him, and said, *"Lo siento, señor, cuando me saluda, estaba pensando en otras cosas y no respondí."*("I am sorry, sir when you wished me; I was thinking about other things and failed to respond.") *"No se preocupe. Tenga un buendia."* ("Don't worry, Sir. Have a good day.") I smiled back and said, *"Usted tambien tenga un buen dia."* (You too have a good day!) As I got in my car, the driver smiled at me and said, "That was nice of you!" I smiled back. A lesson learned.

We reached the city of Antigua. It was another beautiful colonial town. My driver said that he would go back and return at 4 PM in the evening and he put me along with the tourists visiting the volcanoes. We drove down to one of the volcanoes and trekked up the crater. The ground was black as soot; the fumes coming out from the base of the rocks smelt of sulphur. Our guide gave each one of us a marshmallow and we barbecued it on those hot stones. On our way back, we drove around some more volcanoes. I was amazed to watch some of them emit fumes.

I reached Antigua early and took a walk, exploring the colonial wonder. It was getting late, the tourists started to leave for Guatemala City, and I was left alone. The driver had promised to arrive at four, and it was six now, and yet there was no sign of him. My passport was at the homestay and I had forgotten to carry the address with me. Though there was a lurking fear in me, I started to think with a composed mind on what would be my next course of action. I was contemplating going to the local police to inform them of my situation and leave the task of finding my homestay to them. With the tourists gone, the city wore a deserted look. I found a coffee shop and continued to wait. I was worried as I had some cash on me and the driver was nowhere near. My mind was searching for a solution. I took a walk to find out if there was a lodge to stay for the night and also a cyber café to check my mails so that I could trace my homestay booking. It was 7 PM in the night, and out of the blue, I heard a honk. At last, my taxi had arrived. It was a huge relief to see the driver. He apologised for his late arrival and was explaining what went wrong. It didn't matter; I felt safe. I got in the car and went back to my homestay.

The next day late in the night, I took a bus to Flores. It was an overnight ride on the bus. Flores is a beautiful town on an island in a lake connected to the mainland by a short causeway. A gateway to the Mayan ruins, the city itself is a tourist site with elegant colonial buildings and cobble paved roads. I checked into a hotel and immediately went off to Tikal, an ancient Mayan citadel ensconced amid the rain forests of Guatemala. One of the world's heritage sites, it is known for its biodiversity and archeological importance. Possibly inhabited from the 6th century BC, the Tikal complex consists of citadels, palaces, temples, and city squares. The structures and the layout give us a glimpse of the rich ancient civilisation which spreads up to Mexico. After a visit to the adjacent National park, I returned to Flores to enjoy my evening in one of the cosy bars.

Next in line was Belize, a Central American country sharing coast with the Caribbean Sea. It was from Flores that I took a flight to Belize City. Initially, I was not allowed to board as I didn't have a visa. I insisted and persuaded them that with a US visa, I could get to Belize. Reluctantly the airlines permitted me to fly in their small seven-seater aircraft. On arrival, the immigration stopped me from entering for not having a visa. I explained to the officers and showed a piece of information printed from the internet that no permit was needed if one had a US visa. They made me wait while they checked with the back office. In the meanwhile, I made some friends among the officers there. They were quite amiable. They welcomed me to their office and offered me coffee and snacks. They even gave me some tips on travelling in Belize and warned me not to venture out at night. While I was talking with them, my approval from the office had come, and I was free to enter the country.

I had already planned to spend three days in Caye Caulker Island, so I directly took a taxi to the ferry station and boarded a water taxi to the island on the Caribbean Sea. Caye Caulker is a small narrow strip of land of just eight kilometers in length and a kilometer and a half wide. An hour of boat ride later, I landed on the island and checked into my cottage by the sea. Caye Caulker was a lazy laid back island free from all vehicular traffic with some souvenir shops, bicycle rentals, swimming accessories rentals, bars, and local roadside barbeque joints. One of the best beaches I had ever set foot on, I used to spend the day sitting in a high chair sipping beers and eating lobsters from the roadside barbeques. I even signed up for snorkeling, and I, along with an American couple, took a boat and went into the sea. The beauty of the island is that a few miles from the island is the Belize Barrier Reef – the second largest coral reef in the world which runs for around 300 kilometers, I guess. As the waves break at the reef, the sea at the island resembles a massive lake with no waves. It was a perfect spot to snorkel. The underwater marine world is another spectacularly breathtaking experience. The colours of the corals and shells, the different marine organisms with different hues, the school of fish which whiz past you, coupled with the deafening silence of the waters make it a coruscating experience. At another spot, we could find nurse sharks, stingrays, and other fishes, but this time we were watching from the boat.

The island was an unforgettable spectacle for me. It was a never before experience where I would sit for hours on the beach, silently watching the still blue sea. The vision of the vast, endless sea and the pleasant breeze was a soothing balm to the dynamic mind. Sitting quietly and doing nothing but just watching, thinking about nothing is another amazing out of the world experience. Again Mother Nature taught me how to experience happiness through the stillness of the blank mind.

The last of my South American trip was to visit Chichen Itza – another one of the Seven Wonders of the World. From Caye Caulker Island, I took a boat to Chetumal in Mexico. On arrival, the Mexican Customs entered the boat for inspection, and then we were asked to leave our bags on the floor and stand aside. The sniffer dogs would come and sniff us and our baggage for recreational contraband and once they gave the nod, we humans were allowed to go through immigration. Chetumal is a rusty town. I shared a taxi with a co-traveller and reached the Bus station to board a bus to Cancun. The journey to Cancun was about 7 hours, and as usual, I spent the time watching the Mexican countryside.

On arrival at Cancun, I checked-in at a resort on the beach. It was a large property with a private beach. Food and drinks were on the house, meaning they had already charged the whole thing beforehand. It was a comfortable and pleasant stay. The next day, the resort management, arranged a trip for travellers to visit the complex of Mayan ruins at Chichen Itza. The *El Castillo* or the Step Pyramid is a massive structure of ruins and a significant attraction. Another impressive structure is the ball court, probably used for sports activity. The walls of the court depict sculptures of the victors holding the severed heads of the losers. Apart from these, there are many structures in the complex, namely, the *Casa Colorado*, temple of the bearded man, temple of skulls, *El Caracol*, and the temple of warriors. There is this place called the *Cenote Ik Kil* or a swimming pool in a cave, open to the sky. The hanging vines cascading into the waters make a spectacular view. Even if one rushes through the sites, it would take a whole day. Such is the magnitude of the complex.

Finishing my South American tour with Cancun, Mexico, I boarded a flight to Houston and from there to Las Vegas. This South American trip has had a significant impact on me. Within a month I visited ten countries, saw three of the Seven Wonders of the World, tasted different cuisines, and met different people. There were these ancient architectural wonders like the Machu Picchu, Mayan complexes in Tikal and Chichen Itza, and also the modern twisted tower in Panama, which left me enthralled. There were these beaches, forests, swamps, volcanoes, and deep seas, which equally captivated and enchanted me. There were many things on this trip which left a remarkable influence on me, which in due course, changed my personality to a great extent. I learned from these Latin countries to be friendly with strangers, smile, and wish them. I had learned the values of courteousness and politeness from my experience at a Brazilian Airport. I was made aware of the importance of respecting a fellow human being by a Guatemalan driver. When I am wrong, I learned to shed ego and apologise, irrespective of the person's stature.

Through my trip and through my interaction with the Latin people, I understood that poverty might be economical but not psychological. You are poor only if you chose to be. I learned the concept of enjoying life from the Latinos as the only purpose of life is to live happily. Finally, the one good quality which this South American trip taught me is to listen – listen to people, listen to your heart, and listen to nature's voice.

I landed in Houston as a better human being. After meeting Saravanan and his family, I cleared my Immigration formalities and went in search of food. It was a long flight and I was desperate to eat my fill when I heard a woman's voice say, "Sir, your Hindu non-vegetarian meal." as she handed over the food tray with a smile.

X

The food was delicious, and the dessert, impressive! I checked my watch, and in another three hours, I would land in Istanbul. The young lady next to me inquired, "What happened to you? You seem to be immersed in your thoughts most of the time."

I smiled and said, "Nothing like that. I just took a short nap. When I was awake, you were sleeping, and probably when you were awake, I was sleeping."

She smiled and said, "In another three hours we would be in Istanbul and we have an immediate flight to Moldova, so we have to run as soon as we land."

I assured them, "Shouldn't be a worry. You will catch the flight. I guess yours is a connecting flight, isn't it?

She responded immediately, "Yes, it is."

"Then there is no problem. They would need time to shift the baggage from this flight, and in the meantime, you can make it to your flight to Moldova." I reassured.

I then went on to ask, "If you don't mind, what was the language you guys were conversing in?"

She said, "It's Russian. Though the majority speaks Romanian, they do speak Russian in our country." While she was replying, I could see the joy in her eyes. It is quite natural to be excited when someone talks about your culture or nation.

I asked, "Do they speak English in Moldova?" She frowned a bit and said, "In the capital city Chişinău, yes, most of them speak... but in other cities and towns like Soraca from where I come, they don't."

"So, a tourist will have a tough time exploring your country if he doesn't know Russian or Romanian?" She chuckled and said, "Should be... Yes, it would be difficult." and she continued, "Once a couple of friends came down from the US to visit us and they said they would go and explore the town. I was busy but I offered to send someone along with them to assist, but they said they could manage and left. They returned in the evening exhausted, and their first complaint was, 'Why don't these guys speak English? We had trouble communicating everywhere.' I laughed and told them, 'You should have listened to me.' Anyway, it was an experience, wasn't it?"

I said, "Yep, it was an experience. I, too, had one!"

Her eyes wide with astonishment, she asked, "Is that true? Where was it?" She leaned forward to listen to my story.

I said, "China." She immediately said, "Wow! China! You've been there! That's amazing!", unable to control her eagerness.

I said, "Yes" and I continued. "It was in Hangzhou, China. I landed at the airport and had very little

Chinese Renminbi in hand. I was reluctant to exchange my US dollars at the airport as the exchange rate was suicidal. I decided to exchange my precious currency at the Hangzhou Railway Station from where I was supposed to catch a bullet train to Shanghai. Whatever Chinese currency I had, I used it to pay for the taxi to drop me at the train station, and I had no Chinese money left to purchase my ticket. I looked around and there was no sign of a money exchange centre. The station was a busy area with lots of people commuting. I stopped to ask people where I could find a money exchange centre but none could understand my language. They just nodded and walked off busily. I then took out a dollar note and showed the passersby that I would want to exchange the currency. I tried all sorts of sign languages. They would just step back and walk away. Probably they were under the impression that I was trying some trick on them. I sat down at a corner for 15 minutes. At last, I found a policeman went straight to him and asked, "'Do you speak English?'" I then picked my dollar note and enacted the same sign language. At least the policeman understood that I needed help. He stood next to me and started asking the passersby whether they spoke English. It was after 10 minutes that one gentleman said yes, and when I talked to him in English and explained that I needed to exchange money. He didn't speak a word but just showed me a bank behind and asked me to go there and exchange. I felt like a clown, standing in front of the bank and doing all kinds of gestures. All I should have done was to turn back and look. I thanked the policeman *'xie xie'* – the only Mandarin word I knew and walked into the bank."

Both the ladies burst into laughter, imagining my plight. The elderly lady asked me, "So tell me where all did you go and how was it travelling without knowing the language?"

I said, "It was a wonderful experience, in fact!" and continued. "After getting into the bullet train which was an amazing ride, of course, I reached Shanghai. The problem now was to reach my hotel. Thoughtfully, I had taken a print of my hotel reservation and it had the address printed in Mandarin. I showed it to a policeman stationed there, who took me to the metro train station and told the person on the ticket counter to give a ticket for the area of the hotel. He then took me to the platform and with sign language, he told me to get down at the 7th stop. I understood immediately as, by then, I had quickly become an expert in sign language. My problem didn't end when I reached the local destination. I had to find my street and building. It was a repeat show again, showing the address to passersby to help me. Eventually, I reached my hotel after a walk of a kilometer or so. I had already lost my patience. I asked the hotelier to arrange for a sightseeing tour and he readily showed me a package. I did the tour of the Oriental pearl tower, Yu garden, and the cruise. From Shanghai, I took a flight to Beijing."

I continued, sipping water from my bottle, "Beijing was a different experience altogether. I stayed close to Tiananmen Square, which is also near to the Forbidden City. The Forbidden City was a palace of the Ming dynasty, and it is a must-visit place." The younger lady started to ask, and before she could, I interrupted, "I know you were going to ask about the Great Wall, isn't it?" She said, "Yes!" I could see the spark of interest in her eyes.

"Of course, I did visit the Great Wall. It is something you have to see for yourself. You can walk on the wall, and in some places, it is so low, you can climb with ease. I was on a local tour of the Great Wall and along with me were a few travellers from Europe. Much more than the tour, the guides were interested in selling things to us. First, they took us to a silk factory and they explained the way the Silk fabric was processed. They somehow convinced me, a person coming from a hot city, to buy a silk quilt, which was usually used by people hailing from colder climates. They are excellent salesmen. Next, they took me to a tea factory and showed me the different Chinese teas, and again I ended up buying myself a box of tea. By the way, I am a coffee lover. After the long walk at the wall, they took us to a healing centre that gave us a soothing foot massage. These salesmen then came out with Chinese medicines, but this time I ran away and sat in my tour van. I was on a thrifty tour, and I felt these salesmen were hell-bent upon selling all of their merchandise to me and make me walk to India."

Both the ladies burst out into uncontrollable laughter. I then continued, "In Beijing again, I had an experience where my ignorance of the Mandarin language put me in a fix, causing me to lose money. I went to a small beer joint near the Forbidden City and asked for a beer. The person brought me a big menu card printed in the Chinese language and asked me to choose from it.

I saw a picture of Heineken beer and asked him to get one for me. When the check arrived, it was nearly $25. I was shocked. I said that I had asked for one beer and you charged me $25! He said, you showed me this and this is the price for that. Unable to enter into a fight, I paid my $25 and to balance out, I had to cut short my other expenses."

The ladies again started to laugh as though they were listening to their favourite comedy show. "So it was only Shanghai and Beijing you went to?" the younger one asked. I said, "No, from Beijing, I went to Xi'an. I was there for two days. It is famous for the terracotta soldiers. I went to the archeological site where excavations unearthed the terracotta army of the Emperor. From Xi'an, I flew to Shenzhen at the Hong Kong border. This city is known for its shopping destinations. I visited a few malls where you can buy hordes of hardware, pen drives, and other electronic goods at throwaway prices. I also happened to visit the Window of the World centre, which has the entire world's landmarks in miniatures. It was a good experience. From Shenzhen, I took a metro and reached Hong Kong. I spent a few days visiting the Tian Tan Buddha, Victoria Peak, Madame Tussauds, and the city skyline in the evenings. From there, I took a boat to Macau, spent a day, and flew back home."

The ladies seemed to be fascinated listening about my tour and asked me, "I am sure that would have been an unforgettable trip." I said, "Of course, it was an unforgettable experience. Travelling through a country that doesn't speak your language is quite an experience. I was amazed by the cities of China, their tall skyscrapers, and the orderliness. Just like India is known as a country of snake charmers to the western world, I always imagined China as a country of Shaolin fighters and people in the Mao suit, Tang suit, and *Qipao*. In reality, I have not seen a snake charmer in India for years. If you spot a snake charmer in India, you would most likely see the locals themselves surrounding him and watching in awe. Those days of snake charmers are gone. Similarly, what I imagined of China and what I saw were entirely different. China is more of a modern country with underlying traditional values; everything about China seems to be methodical, systematic, and orderly."

I smiled at the ladies who were by then in awe of my travel story. At that moment, I heard the announcement, "Please fasten your seat belts and close your tray tables as we would be landing shortly at the Istanbul International Airport." It was then we realised that my Chinese travel story killed three hours of our journey. In a few moments, the flight descended at Istanbul and it was a smooth touchdown. A few passengers clapped their hands for the perfect landing. The flight slowed down and taxied to its destined bay. Once the seat belt sign was switched off, all the impatient passengers got up at once to pick up their hand baggage. They were not ready to waste a single minute more on the flight. Handbags in their hand, all were waiting for the doors to open, and it was like an "On your marks, get, set, go" kind of situation waiting for the gun to go. The elderly lady went and picked up the bridal dress and was ready to bid farewell to me. The younger one said, "It was nice to know you and fun talking.

The world is small; we would surely bump again somewhere and someplace in the future." I said, "Yes, true. Who knows, we would surely meet up somewhere! But that time I'll make sure that I stalk you." and I smiled. The ladies laughed and walked away to the front, squeezing themselves through the passengers to catch their flight to Moldova.

I sauntered ahead, dragging my bag as I had another 4 hour wait to board my next flight to New Delhi. I checked the departure notice board, confirmed my flight boarding gate, and started walking towards it.

XI

Istanbul International Airport was quite big and I had to cover a fair distance to get to the departure gate for my flight to New Delhi. On the way, I found a restroom, washed my face, and despite that, the weariness of the long journey was still there. I then realised that I was famished and started to look for a restaurant to taste some Turkish food. Before I could find a Turkish restaurant, I found Burger King and ordered myself a burger with some French fries as I couldn't wait to eat.

Istanbul is famous for its cuisine and is one of the world's renowned food destinations. On my way to Bogota, Colombia, had cut short my journey especially to spend a few days in this historic city of Istanbul. I have read a lot about this city since my school days - that it was first known as Constantinople, and later Istanbul. Over a period of time, I had developed a lot of interest and the city made its way to my bucket list. When I said that I would be travelling to Istanbul, my friend Vinod, who travels a lot for work, had given me a metro-card and told me to use the card for my local city tour. I took accommodation in Sultan Ahmet, which is a tourist area and close to the famous Blue Mosque and a tram station. Once settled in my hotel, I went up to the tram station to recharge my metro-card. Instead of adding 10 Turkish liras, I topped up 100 liras by mistake, which was equivalent to around USD 135. Cursing myself for the stupid mistake, I walked back to my hotel. It was a festival day, *Eid-ul-Bakrid*, and there wasn't much crowd. When I reached the hotel, I sat down with the receptionist, a girl in her early 20s, and was telling her how I mistakenly topped 100 liras instead of 10, and I asked her if there was a way to get back a refund. She looked at me, bemused, and said, "Why did you recharge your metro card?" I said, "If I had to go around the city, I had to, didn't I?" She said, "Sir, it is *Eid-ul-Bakrid* - for the next three days, you can travel for free! Why didn't you ask me before recharging your card?" I said, "My fate! I never knew that!" and walked back to my room with a sorrowful face.

I came down after relaxing for an hour and found the girl still at work. She saw me coming down and called me to give me some information. She said, "Sir, it is a good time to visit the Grand Bazaar. Why don't you go there now? But please don't forget to bargain and be careful with your belongings." I thanked her for the useful tip. Probably she didn't want me to lose any more money.

Grand Bazaar is probably the oldest and largest shopping area in the world. Housing more than 4,000 shops, it was a challenging maze. Once you enter, you should keep track of your route, else you may end up exiting out somewhere else. It was a crowded bazaar thronged with people, and there were shops selling carpets, *hookas,* antiques, and other souvenirs. I have a habit of buying fridge magnets depicting the country or the place I visit. As usual, buying a fridge magnet was the only purchase I make. I walked around the shops selected a fridge magnet and asked for its price. The vendor said 30 Euros. It was exorbitant. I moved further to another shop and here the vendor said 25 Euros. I remembered the advice of the girl from the hotel; I immediately put my bargaining skills to use. I said 15, and he said 20, and at last, we settled at 16 Euros. It was a beautiful magnet piece depicting the Hagia Sophia Mosque. Proud of myself for being an astute bargainer and making a kill, I walked back to the hotel. The girl at the desk was still working. I went to her and thanked her for the tip and narrated the whole experience to her. I showed the piece which I bought, feeling proud of my skills. She saw the souvenir and asked me, "Sir, how much did you tell me that you bought this one for?" I said, "He said 25, and I bargained for 16 Euros!" and looked at her with smugness. She stared at me with pity and said, "Please visit the shop next door; you will find the same piece for 5 Euros. I think you have a habit of losing money." The entire aura turned into darkness in a minute. I smacked myself on my face and took the piece from her and said, "Thank you again for this information." How I wish she had never told me about the next door shop and let me enjoy the false feeling of accomplishment as a skilled bargainer!

I dedicated the next day to the Topkapi Palace, the Blue Mosque, and the Hagia Sophia Mosque. The Hagia Sophia, my favourite edifice, was a Church and then was converted into a mosque. Converted to a museum later, it is now a mosque again. After an exhausting day, I went for a Turkish bath. It was in an old building that looked like a bath of the Harappa civilisation days. I was first asked to go into a steam room and then in a small pool with chilled water for a swim. Then came a hefty guy who had a piece of leather in his hand and with some oil and foam he scrubbed off my skin without giving any heed to me. I took a shower next. Once out of the agony of the old-school scrub, it felt like a reincarnation in a different body. From there, I took a tram to a place suggested by a guy from the bath counter to relish the taste of an excellent spicy Turkish cuisine.

Balat was next on the itinerary. It is a delightful neighbourhood and a home for many traditional Jewish and Greek Orthodox families in Istanbul. The beauty of Balat lies in its narrow cobbled streets going up steeply with wooden dwellings on either side, with each house painted in different colours. It was here that I met an Italian couple and together we went to the Fatih Mosque and finished the day with a view from the Galata Tower. In the evening, was a boat ride on the Bosphorus strait, which divides Europe and Asia, to enjoy a splendid view at sunset.

My history books referred to Turkey as the "Sick man of Europe," a reference to the Ottoman Empire, which was on its decline around the time of the Crimean War. Whatever the reasons may be, it never appeared sick to me; it was a land of great cultural heritage and history. The beautiful grand mosques stood testimony to the artistic skills of the people. One evening, I got to hear the *adhan* or the call to prayer from the mosque; it was so resonant in my mind that each day of my stay in Istanbul, I used to look forward to listening to it.

Among all my travels, Turkey holds a special place for its magnificence and splendour.

As I was recollecting my tour of Istanbul, I finished my burger and fries and slowly treaded to my departure gate to find a comfortable place to sit.

XII

I found a row of vacant seats at some distance from the departure gate and chose one with a perfect vantage point to the entrance. The departure became crowded as passengers started trickling in. Sitting comfortably, I was looking at the other passengers. Some were hurrying and some ambling, enjoying the window shopping. Families were seated in groups and they had a few brats who were always on the lookout to do something naughty. Some passengers were absorbed in their laptops and conveyed an exaggerated occupied status. Probably they were busy with their office work. Never in my life have I been as busy as to take my work along to places I go. Maybe these people are travelling on an assignment. Or perhaps they are busy playing Candy Crush under the pretence of work! Who knows!

Twenty hours of travel was eventually taking a toll on my body. It was craving a cosy bed to lie down and sleep even though my mind was active. I was asking myself why my body wasn't cooperating. Was it because of me getting older by the day or was it that I pampered my body too much with luxury? I remember the days when I had embarked on a religious trip with my friend Mathi and I would drive myself all through without giving the wheels to him. I never felt tired. Also, the 15 day road trip with my brother-in-law, Segar, came to my mind where again, I always used to snatch an opportunity to drive, and that too never made me feel tired. Of course, they were thrilling trips, so the thought of tiredness never occurred. My mind started to drift to the road trip, reminiscing the beautiful experience and the electrifying exhilaration.

It all started over a drink in Singapore with my brother-in-law Segar. He was narrating his road trip from Singapore to Bangkok and I was very eager to take one. I asked him, "Why don't we take one like that?" He said, "Sure, why don't we plan something different? Why don't we do it in the US?" I said, "That would be awesome!" He declared, "So let's do it in the US! Get ready for route 66!"

Route 66 is a highway cutting across the US from Chicago to Santa Monica. It was the first all-weather highway, running from Chicago, through Missouri, Kansas, Oklahoma, Texas, New Mexico, and Arizona before ending in Santa Monica, California and covering a distance of around 3,940 km. I started to make a note of the route and its history, and Segar made a perfect plan to execute.

The day we landed in Chicago, we hired a Chevrolet Cruze and retired to our motel to relax for the day. The next day, we went around the city visiting tourist sites like the Art Institute of Chicago, Millennium Park, Buckingham Fountain, and the 360 Chicago. The 360 Chicago is an Observation Deck on the 94th floor of the John Hancock Building. The glass walls and height of the observatory gives a breathtaking view of the city. The next day we drove down to Michigan Lake and spent some time enjoying the breeze and the rather chilly weather. It was the first week of June, and the weather was still icy chill. We finished our tour of the city and reached Adam's street where we started our Route 66 journey from the signboard which read "Route 66 Begin."

After taking photographs, we commenced our journey to Springfield, IL. It was almost a four hour drive to the city. On the way, we stopped at the "Dell Rhea Chicken Basket" to taste some chicken, and we had the Route 66 beer, which was nothing but a regular nonalcoholic root beer, christened after the road. Visiting the Abraham Lincoln Cemetery, we stopped at Ambler's Texaco Gas Station at Dwight IL, which was the oldest serving gas station on Route 66. No longer in operation, it is now a roadside attraction. When we went there, it was closed. Watching us waiting, an old lady in her 80s came to us with the keys and opened up the station for us. While conversing with her, I got to know that she spends her time helping to maintain the station as it was her town's pride. She was proud of her soil and very enthusiastically explained the days of the station as she had known since her childhood. Thanking her for her courteousness, we drove to Springfield, IL, to retire for the day. We had covered our first 340 kilometers for the day.

Springfield, the capital of Illinois, boasts of being home to Abraham Lincoln till he became the President of the country. We visited Lincoln's home and the Lincoln-Herndon law offices before leaving the city. From Springfield, it was on to Rolla,

Missouri, a distance of roughly 350 km. En route, we visited St. Louis and had a peep at the iconic gateway arch. As the road was closed for repairs, we had to take a detour into the city. It was in the bypass that we spotted the monument. Had there been no ongoing repairs, we would have driven straight through and would have missed it. From St. Louis, it was a straight drive to Rolla, MO. We reached there early, did some shopping, and also visited the Stonehenge, a local attraction of the town. The following day was a Sunday, and Segar, being a Christian, went to pray at the local Methodist Church. I took the time to visit the Laundromat to wash our clothes. It was there I met another old lady in her late 80s who had also come for the Laundromat. I introduced myself and told her that I was on a road trip on route 66. While we were waiting for our clothes to be washed and dried, she started reminiscing about some exciting incidents which happened in her younger days when she went on a road trip. It was a story which had happened sixty years ago. She was on a road trip with her boyfriend, who took her on a ride in his newly purchased car. They drove deep into the woods when the car broke down. They were absolutely clueless about the mechanism of the vehicle and were scared to walk back home as they were a few miles into the woods. They stayed in the car for the next two days, solely surviving on a bottle of water. It was only when her dad, along with his folks, found them and they were able to go home. I asked her about the boyfriend and she quickly retorted, "Do you think that old bastard would have survived till now? He must be sleeping somewhere deep under." She was witty and it was fun chatting with her. Once Segar returned, I took my leave of the old lady and started off to our next destination, Miami, Oklahoma.

The drive to Miami, OK, was a picturesque one. On the way at Springfield, OK, we stopped to see a natural wonder called the Fantastic Caverns. It is a natural cave formation formed thousands of years ago and is probably one of the few drive-through caves where a van driven wagon takes the tourists on a 50 minute drive. The Stalactites and the Stalagmites in the cave enthralled me and reminded me of Steven Spielberg's Hollywood flick, *The Raiders of the Lost Ark*. There was also a small trail that took 30 minutes of our time and it was a joyful walk through the rocky terrain. We then drove onward to Miami, OK, clocking a distance of around 400 km for the day.

Miami, OK, not to be confused with Miami, Florida, is a charming town with beautiful lamp-posts, banners, and arches. The town took pride in the highway and celebrated it through banners and posts. We visited the famous Coleman theatre of 1929, which was a noted landmark of Miami and is now known as the Miami Convention and Visitors Bureau. From Miami, our next destination was to Elk City, OK. It was a long drive of 500 plus kilometers, but we happened to pass through many attractions on the way. We first visited an old gas station from the 1930s at Afton, OK which had an annex displaying a variety of vintage cars. The next was Ed Galloway's Totem Pole Park near Foyel, OK. Constructed with tons of sand, rock cement, and steel, this Totem Pole was the world's largest. It depicted paintings and patterns of Native American culture. Our next stop en route was Tulsa, a city on the Arkansas River in Oklahoma. Here we visited an exciting place called the Center of the Universe, downtown. It is a structure with a small concrete circle on the floor, surrounded by larger circles of bricks. It is a mysterious acoustics phenomenon where you stand in the middle of the ring facing any direction and make a noise - the sound comes back to you much more amplified. We stood there making noises like children, and once done, it was a straight drive to Elk City, OK, where we rested for the night.

We left Elk City quite early as it was going to be a long drive to Tucumcari, New Mexico, a distance of about 500 km. We passed through Shamrock, which again had an old gas station on the 66, and entered Texas. Before arriving in Amarillo, TX, we visited Jack Sisemore's RV Museum which exhibits a vintage collection of trailers, campers, and mobile homes dating back to the 1930s. At Amarillo, we stopped at the Cadillac Ranch, a public art installation consisting of 10 Cadillacs buried nose-first in the ground. As a ritual, the tourists coming there spray some paint on those cars and make them more colourful. The day ended with our stay at a motel in Tucumcari, NM.

Tucumcari is a small town in New Mexico with a population of around 5,000. It is a beautiful town with motels, colourful shops, and of course, a Route 66 museum. From Tucumcari, we first drove to Santa Fe NM, the capital of New Mexico State. The beauty of the city lies in its buildings built in a traditional method with sun-dried mud and straw. The earth or clay used for plastering made the walls look reddish-brown, and this gave a different hue to the cities and towns in New Mexico. We visited the Heritage Center, the Cathedral, and the oldest trading post established in 1605. By late night we reached Grants NM after driving a distance of 500 km.

The following day was an exciting drive. On our way to Winslow, Arizona, we first visited the El Malpais National Conservation Area. The area is full of sandstone cliffs and canyons with extreme barren lands and is a perfect place for trekking. The natural arch formed by the rocks called La Ventana Natural Arch is a great visual spectacle. We also visited the big skylight cave in the area. Though a bit challenging to access, I did not want to miss the chance to view the irresistible natural wonder. It was a natural cave in the ground and I walked my way deep down while balancing myself between the rocks and treading through the rugged path. After a strenuous trek of a few meters, I found myself in a spacious area. High above me, I saw an opening that spilled to the sky, and what I saw was baffling. The light coming from above formed a spectacular view and was a photographer's delight. I was stunned; it was like rays descending from the heavens to the dark earth. I stood there silently, feeling the chillness of my sweat, smelling the moisture of the rocks, and viewing the picturesque scene. I was, for a moment, in union with nature. I thanked God for the beautiful experience and headed back with contentment. An hour's drive from there took us to the El Morro National Monument. Rising high above the valley floor was this colossal sandstone cliff. We walked around the area on the pedestrian track, laid down by the authorities, and explored the terrain. Enjoying the drive, we reached Winslow, AZ, after a ride of around 500 km. Once we checked-in at a motel, we went to a nearby store to pick something for dinner when I heard someone call me.

XIII

"Sir! Sir! Here you are! I was looking for you near the departure gate". I was staring at the person with my mind in Winslow, AZ. I jumped back to my senses in a few seconds and I realised that it was the Indian IT guy from Dallas. I shook my head and said, "Yeah, hey! There was too much crowd at the gate so I found this place here." and further asked "Are you flying to Delhi?" He said, "Yeah, of course! It is a connecting flight to New Delhi and from there I'll catch the morning flight to Bangalore." "Oh, ok!" I replied. This guy was alone and had no one to talk to and must be feeling bored. He then said, "We have another 2 hours for departure. Shall we go and get something to eat?" he invited. "No, buddy, I just had my food, and I am feeling a bit tired; I want to relax. You carry on. Thanks for the invitation." I said. Lest I forget, I said, "Bro, when they announce departure, just wake me up in case I fall asleep." He said, "Sure, better relax, we have another 6 hours of flight." He walked away to find a restaurant. I was watching the guy leave and slowly my mind slipped back to Winslow, AZ.

Winslow to Kingman, AZ was just around 350 km, so we started late, and after passing Seligman, where we stopped for gas, we reached Kingman quite early. We checked into a motel and there we met a Telugu Indian family from Visakhapatnam, Andhra Pradesh. The man was an English teacher and had got a job in Texas. His wife and two kids had just joined him and they were on a road trip when their car broke down. They, too, checked into the same motel. They were asking the reception desk for help when we walked in. Segar helped them with making calls to a car repair service and also offered to drive the gentleman to a nearby supermarket for food and other stuff. His wife was an orthodox lady who always carried an electric stove and other utensils to cook on their journey. She invited us for dinner where we had authentic home-cooked Indian food after a long time. We spent the evening talking to them and retired late.

Kingman, AZ, a city on Route 66, had a lot of attractions to offer. Prominent among those were the Route 66 museum and the locomotive museum which displayed locomotive engines from the past century. From here, we were supposed to go to Barstow, CA, but Segar wanted a detour as Las Vegas was close by, just a hop away at 240 km. So we drove past Dolan Springs, Hoover Dam, and reached Las Vegas and checked-in at the Mandalay Bay Hotel. Segar went off to try his luck at the Casino and I went off to sleep.

The next two days were spent in Las Vegas, pampering ourselves in the hotels and the bars. We also went on a drive to Mount Charleston, which is at a distance of about 65 km from Vegas. It was the perfect place for camping and trekking. The weather was cold and the drive was pleasant. The following day was enjoyable too. We started off to drive the next 330 km to Barstow, CA, and en route, we had to pass through the Mojave Desert. It was a slight detour but the experience was terrific. The road to the desert was brown concrete and deserted. We couldn't see a vehicle or any human in the vicinity. We parked our car and walked into the desert. The path was full of cactus plants, or should I say trees, as they were taller than me. The silence of the desert was deafening, only occasionally interrupted by the sound of the wind. I also happened to hear a hissing sound and a hustle in the bush very close to me; guessing it could be a rattlesnake, I ran back to my car to drive down to Barstow. My heart was thumping for a while. Luckily it was not my day to die and that too, not a solitary death in the desert.

Barstow is a big town, and along with the usual Route 66 Museum, it has got the Western American Railroad Museum, which shares the history of railroading in the Pacific Southwest. After spending the night in the town, we continued the following day, which brought us to the last day of our road trip from Barstow to Santa Monica. As it was the last day of our drive, I was a bit sad as the experience and the enjoyment was coming to an end. But the journey still had something in store for me. While having breakfast at our motel, we learned about a place called Calico Ghost Town from one of the travellers. We decided to visit even though the town was in the opposite direction of our route. It was a 20 km drive to the town and we had to park our car at some distance and enter. Calico Ghost Town was an abandoned and an old West mining town. The town was converted into a park and hence the name Calico Ghost Town.

The abandoned town gives a feel of being in the Wild West of the 19th century. It has a fire hall, town hall, Sheriff's office, a saloon, a beer garden, a hotel, and all the detailing you find in a Clint Eastwood's Wild West movies. I spent an hour going around each of the places, visualising how life would have been then. Would they hang criminals here in front of the town hall? Would they put up posters on these walls announcing bounty to those who bring in the thugs? Had these places witnessed pistol fights? My imagination knew no bounds. After walking backward a century through time, we drove forward to Los Angeles.

We reached Los Angeles quite early and after relaxing for a while, we drove down to Santa Monica, CA, to wrap up our tour. Santa Monica is a busy coastal city facing the Pacific Ocean. We took a walk on the Santa Monica Pier, which was crowded with tourists. On the pier was a signboard - "Santa Monica 66 End of the Trail". We stood there and took a photograph each for future remembrance and to officially finish off our road trip. We were lucky to be there by evening to witness a glorious sunset. The sun was going down the Pacific, making the waters glitter, creating a golden halo around the signboard, which seemed to me like nature's signature symbolising the end of an incredible road journey.

A fortnight earlier, starting from Chicago, we crisscrossed the United States, passing through different states, cities, terrains, weather conditions, meeting people with different accents, and at last set foot in Santa Monica, covering a distance of around 4,000 km. It was a different experience altogether. We visited memorials, went through caverns, walked down the caves, trailed in the desert, ran away hearing the hissing sound, gambled in Vegas, relived the Wild West, and much more. What else could I ask for?

The USA is a country replete with natural abundance. Be it canyons, gorges, coastline beaches, rivers, caves, forests, deserts - it has it all. I was blessed to see, though not all, but a significant majority of it. A nation is known and well understood through its countryside. This journey had taken me deep inside the country and I had had the opportunity to see the United States in its rawness. The towns in the counties took pride in their heritage and culture. The cities along the route celebrated the legacy of highway 66. How the tourist sites and conservation centres are maintained speaks a lot about the people and the love they have for their country and the pride in being Americans. The people, too, were friendly and ever ready to help. Had it not been for their suggestions, we would have missed out most of the attractions.

It was the next day that I flew out of Los Angeles to India and Segar to Singapore. On my flight back, I had an American sitting next to me. While conversing with him, I told him that I had come to make a road trip on Route 66 and also told him about my previous trip to the US when I had visited the east coast. He was awestruck. He said, "I doubt if any average American would have gone around America like you!" I smiled at him and there was a tinge of pride and satisfaction in my smile.

I opened my eyes; the Dallas guy was seated next to me reading a magazine. The airline staff had arrived at the departure gate and was getting ready to announce the departure. The Dallas guy smiled at me and we started walking to the departure gate to join the boarding line.

XIV

The departure, as usual, was announced zone wise and my Dallas friend was the first to go. He promised to meet me inside and walked towards the aerobridge after verification at the gate. A few minutes later, I walked into the aircraft receiving the customary welcome from the crew with folded hands. It was easy locating my seat as it wasn't far from the entry door. Thanks to the lady at the departure counter in Miami, I sat at the window seat near the emergency exit. The seats next to me were vacant. This time, I neither wished nor prayed for the place to remain unoccupied as I could tell from the crowd that it was going to be a full flight, and my making wishes would be futile. Before I could settle in, a young couple came and claimed those seats.

The couple would have been in their mid-20s, and the way they were talking and laughing, it would be a fairly solid guess for anyone to say that they were newly married. In contrast, there was another couple in their late 30s sitting quietly as though engrossed in the Swan Lake Ballet of Tchaikovsky. Probably they were married a decade earlier. I had occupied the window seat, the middle seat was taken by the lad, and the aisle seat by his wife. The lad was busy talking to his wife and occasionally turning across to me as though to check on what I was doing. I smiled and said, "Hi, How are you?" which I usually do on a flight. That was enough of a trigger to bring out the loquaciousness in him, and he immediately started, "I am Deepak, and this is my wife, Lekha. We got married recently and returning from our honeymoon in Europe. I am from Jaipur, but I have a business in Delhi... " He went on and on revealing all about his native place, his family, his business, and all the other things irrelevant to me. The only thing he failed to disclose was his list of assets and liabilities. By the time he completed giving full information about himself, the flight had already taken off and was cruising midair.

Slowly to keep myself aloof, I picked up a flight magazine placed in front of me and started to flip through the pages to make my neighbour believe that I was busy reading. The first page turned out to be an article about the Sagrada Familia Church in Barcelona, which Turkish Airlines was enticing travellers to visit in their carriers. Deepak saw the picture of the Sagrada Familia and immediately started narrating his visit to the Church with much enthusiasm. He spoke about Spain and was lecturing me that I should visit the country at least once in my life. I nodded my head in approval. I was enjoying the zest and liveliness in him while he kept on bragging about his travel. I could relate to him as I recalled the feeling of narrating the whole voyage to my classmates in school after the annual trip to Trichy with my family. He was continuing nonstop about his journey and the words became less and less audible as my mind started to wade back in memory, reminiscing the days of my European travel.

Though I had travelled to many places in Europe, there is still a lot more left to visit. To be frugal, I planned my trips in small segments so that I could explore Europe at leisure. My first trip started with Barcelona, Spain. With my knowledge of Spanish coming handy, it was relatively easy to communicate, but at times it was difficult when I got caught in the accents. Barcelona airport has a metro train service within the complex making it easy for me to catch the train to reach my hotel. My hotel was next to the metro and a supermarket, so I never had to worry about food or travel. There was this one thing which I learned from my brother-in-law Segar, who would say that I should always make my food purchases at the supermarket, have a substantial breakfast before leaving, skip lunch, and have an early dinner. He would tell me to find Doner Kebab shops, which are in every nook and corner of Europe and have a *shawarma* or a *falafel,* which would be spicy and filling for an Indian traveller. He would also say that once in three days, I can pamper myself with the local cuisine. I religiously follow it to this day.

Barcelona, the capital of Spain's Catalonian region, has many tourist attractions. But the most important ones which caught my attention were the Sagrada Familia Cathedral and the Montjuic Magic Fountain. The Sagrada Familia Cathedral is one imposing and a great architectural wonder. Designed by the Spanish artist Antoni Gaudi, it remains to date incomplete. Being one of the most fantastic attractions in Europe, tourists swarm the place, and there is always a huge line at the entrance. Running short of time, I explored the cathedral from the outside in all possible ways and kept it on my bucket list to visit in my future travels. The Font Magica de Montjuic is in the centre of Plaza Espanya at the foot of The Palau Nacional. The pathway to the Palace was decorated with a series of fountains with huge ones at the centre. There were steps on either side of the path where people sat like in a gallery. At designated times, the fountains sprung to life to opera music. The combination of colours, music, light, motion, and water acrobatics made it a display of extravagance. The waters synced to the tempo of the music, and the jet spout complemented it by throwing water up to 150 feet. It was one enthralling experience.

From Barcelona, it was Paris by train. As is my habit, I found a window seat to watch the city recede and the beautiful European villages to begin. I spent the next six and a half hour journey occasionally drinking coffee from the attached pantry and enjoying the view of the countryside. I reached Paris Gare de Lyon station by evening. It was a huge station and a junction where people interchanged trains. I scrupulously followed the instructions of my host in Paris and reached his place without any hiccups. My host was a friendly Chinese man who allowed me to stay in their home. I had free access to their kitchen. With some bread, eggs, and a few vegetables, I prepared my daily breakfast and a sandwich for the afternoon. Paris is a historic city and I gave myself four days of stay to explore. The city was well connected with the underground metro system, and with Google maps, I never found any difficulty in reaching the desired destinations.

After a good night's rest, I started my day with the Church of Notre Dame on the banks of the Seine

River. A medieval church and a masterpiece of Gothic architecture, Notre Dame, is one of the most visited monuments of Paris. The church is a marvel to behold with the arched exterior support known as flying buttresses, its external statues, gargoyles, and the stained glasses. With the lush green gardens and the Seine River in the backdrop, the church was a visual treat even from a distance.

From Notre Dame, taking a metro, I went to the Louvre Museum, the world's largest museum and a historical monument in itself. On the banks of the River Seine, Louvre is the largest repository exhibiting the great works of the Renaissance. It also displays the royal collection of the French rulers and even a collection of ancient Greek and Roman sculptures. A day wouldn't suffice to see the museum in its entirety. My interest was only to see the *Mona Lisa* and getting to the floor took me an hour. Not being a connoisseur of art and with absolutely no knowledge of this field, my only intention was to see the *Mona Lisa* painting not for its artistic eminence but for its popularity. I have always heard and read about it since the days of my childhood. It took me more than an hour to locate the painting. There was a massive crowd in front of the canvas, probably people like me who just wanted to see and tell the world, "Yes! I have seen the *Mona Lisa!*" I was expecting a giant portrait but it was just half of what I imagined. I stood and took a photograph and then found my way out. It took me nearly half a day just to enter the museum, see the Mona Lisa, and exit. It should by now give a picture of the magnitude of this outstanding museum.

Another metro took me from there to the Eiffel Tower, one of the most iconic Seven Wonders of the World. It was a few hundred meters from the metro station to the tower, and as I was walking, I could see the peak of the Eiffel Tower. Once I entered the complex, I was spellbound by its magnificence. This massive wrought iron lattice tower was built for the World Fair and coincidentally to commemorate the 100 years of the French Revolution. I purchased tickets to reach the observatory deck on the third floor. It was a breathtaking view from there. I could see the beautiful city with modern structures interspersed with the old ones. The Seine River flowing around was bracketed at places by beautiful bridges. I stayed back there till it was dark so that I could have a feel of watching the lights decorate the tower at night. This time I moved to the opposite side of the tower to enjoy the view from a different angle. Paris, they say, is a romantic city, and I understood why. The beautiful lights which illuminate the city and the Seine River, which resembles a *sautoir* on a gorgeous *mademoiselle,* gives a passionate feel, and all I missed that day was a sweetheart by my side. After the incredible experience, it was time for me to see the grandeur and splendour of Moulin Rouge!

The birthplace of the modern Can-Can dance, Moulin Rouge, is an old French Cabaret place that opened up in the same year as the Eiffel Tower. I booked my place at the Moulin for the 11 PM show and was there by 10 PM. It was already bustling with people taking photographs of the century-old complex which had a red windmill on its roof. After our tickets were verified, I waited in line to enter. A few minutes before the show, we were allowed to enter, and they seated people on tables which accommodated not more than four. I sat with an American couple who were on a holiday. My ticket entitled me to half a bottle of champagne, which was placed on the table along with a full bottle for the American couple. It was a mesmerising show with beautiful girls presenting an excellent choreography in tune with the music. It was a spectacle of colours, grandeur, and lights. The show was intercepted with talk shows and comedy. I sipped my champagne throughout the two and a half hour show. The American couple put up a stern face all through the show and except for the initial pleasantries, we never had a conversation. Throughout the show, I could sense that their mind was preoccupied with something and they never seemed to appreciate the show. Through the corner of my eye, I could see that they hadn't even touched their bottle. A few minutes before the show could get over, the couple left the place in a hurry, and I had a bottle and a half of champagne on the table at my disposal. Unable to imagine the liquid going down the drain, I drained it into my mouth instead, and by the time I left the hall, I was a bit too intoxicated. It was past midnight and the metro services had ceased to operate. I took a taxi, asked the driver, who was a Lebanese, to show me the city by night and then drop me at my place. He gave me a beautiful ride, taking me through the Champs-Elysees, the Arch of Triumph, Grand Palace, Petit Palace, and the grand fountain at the Place de la Concorde before dropping me at my place.

I was supposed to get up early and take the morning train to Versailles, the famous palace which was once the Royal residence. I had read that the Palace is a vast premise and would take not less than a day to see. By the time I woke up, it was 1 PM. Thanks to the champagne at Moulin Rouge, my day got ruined. Still not losing heart, I ran to the train station and waited for a while to get on a train to Versailles. By the time I reached Versailles, it was 4 PM, and from there, it was a half an hour walk to the palace. It was closing time and I had to satisfy myself by just looking at the magnificent grandeur from the outside. I cursed myself for oversleeping but my sleep had given me another reason to visit France.

On one of my train journeys, I had this jarring experience with French phonetics. French is a sweet language to hear. However, unlike Spanish, French is different and stresses more on phonetics. You don't hear what you see in written, like in Spanish. It was one day when I was travelling on a limited stop train and I had to get down at Bibliothèque François-Mitterrand Station to interchange. Before the stop could arrive, the public announcement said something which I couldn't comprehend. I thought it announced some other stop and I relaxed and waited for my stop's announcement. The station arrived and I was busy looking at the beautiful women entering and leaving. Once the train started to leave, I saw the name of my station go past. I was shocked and got up, but it took another 15 minutes for the next stop to arrive. Being a limited stop train, it didn't stop at some stations. I started counting all the stops in between, so I could correctly get down on my way back. On reaching the station, I crossed over and took another train in the opposite direction and counted my way back to my designated stop, never listening to the public announcement system.

Four days in Paris was an out-of-the-world experience. I was on my own, strolling at a leisurely pace with no one nagging me and with no compulsion to impress anyone or show off. That's one of the benefits you have when you travel solo. You can be as thrifty as possible; there is no one to judge you. You can save tons of money, follow your own routine and timing.

My next destination was to a small village called La Teste-de-Buch located on the southern shore of Arcachon Bay. The purpose was to visit my sister's family which was staying there. My brother-in-law Segar, who works for the Singapore Armed Services, was deputed here at the Cazaux Air Base, and that was reason enough for me to visit Southwest France. It was a three and a half hour train journey from Gare du Nord station, Paris to Bordeaux, and then an hour to La Teste-de-Buch. My sister and Segar were eager to receive me, and the next couple of days, I was at their palatial residence. It was on one of these evenings that I visited the Dune of Pilat, also called the *Grande Dune du Pilat*, the tallest Dune of Europe located at the Arcachon Bay. This dune runs parallel to the shoreline and is an excellent spot for paragliding. Walking my way up to the dune was an enjoyable experience as I got to see the broad view of the humongous sea from a higher plane.

The next day I visited Bordeaux. Just an hour's drive from La Teste-de-Buch, Bordeaux is the wine-growing hub of the region and is dotted with many wineries. We went around the winery to do some wine tasting. I went underground, probably two floors down, to see the barrels and wine casks stored at an apt temperature. It was a new experience. Segar was good at the wine tasting, but for me, everything tasted the same – sweetish bitter. Probably it was an art to master. I bought myself a bottle of wine, and we moved around to see the beauty the city has to offer. Bordeaux is a city of old medieval buildings with cathedrals and palaces. The place which caught my attention was the Place de la Bourse – a square along the Garonne River and a venue for impressive architectural sights. It also features an open plaza with a fountain and a reflecting pool. I could spend hours at this place enjoying its enormity.

With Segar around, there was always some thrill in the offing. Over dinner, he asked me about my plan. I said that I was planning to visit Italy. He then came up with an idea as the week was nearing its end. He suggested that we tour someplace before I fly to Italy. It sounded like a splendid idea and we planned another road trip. He gave me an option. "Either we drive to the French Riviera and the Cannes or Switzerland. It is for you to choose!" I jumped up and said, "This time, we crisscross Switzerland!" It was another tick on my bucket list.

Early one morning, we drove down to Bordeaux, parked our car at the airport, and took a flight to Lyon, France. We hired a car and dashed off to Geneva, which lies in the French-speaking part of Switzerland. It was a two hour drive to reach Geneva. Many books have described this lovely city and I do not have much to add. To put it in a single sentence, it is a city of beauty par excellence. We started with a visit to the century-old fountain – The Geneva Water Fountain, situated on a lake. They say that it is visible throughout the city and is also visible while flying at an altitude of 10 km. The fountain is said to jet water to a height of 140 meters. Next to visit was the floral clock or *L'horloge Fleurie* as it is known. It is an outdoor clock made out of flowers. About 6,500 flowers and shrubs went into the making of the watch, and as seasons change, the flowers do too. We then visited the Reformation Wall - an international monument that depicts important individuals, events, and documents as statues and bas-reliefs, Parc des Bastions – a park with large chess boards and at last the United Nations. A giant broken chair facing the UN complex, which symbolises the campaign against landmines, was another major attraction for the tourists. After finishing our day trip to Geneva, we drove back to France to a place called Chamonix, as staying in Switzerland was very expensive.

Chamonix is a hilly place and a base to get to Mont Blanc. It was a cold night, and as the weather was not conducive, they had suspended the tramway service to Mont Blanc. From Chamonix, we drove to Lausanne. We spent some time at the city's famous lake and also at the 12th century Lausanne Cathedral before leaving for Bern.

Bern, the capital city, lies in the German-speaking part of Switzerland and is not short on tourist attractions. It was around midday when we reached Bern. We parked our car in the old town locality, a medieval area with tall sandstone buildings. As we were exploring the city, we were on a lookout for a McDonald's to fill ourselves with a burger. The search for McDonald's made us traverse the whole of the old town. We walked past the Einsteinhaus, the home to Albert Einstein, through the Zytglogge, a medieval tower with the historic clock installed in 1530, and the Baroque Church of the Holy Spirit before we discovered our McDonald's. Once our hunger was satiated, we took our car and drove past the Bundeshaus or the Swiss Federal Assembly and winded off our day at the German side of the border near Schaffhausen. Again, went there for the same reason - affordable accommodation.

The next day again was a drive into Switzerland to Rhine Falls, Europe's largest plain waterfalls. We went to the Belvedere viewing point, and beneath us, we could see the roaring waters hitting the rocks and spraying foams all the way. It was a stunning view of nature's spectacle. Spending a couple of hours sitting on the bench across and enjoying the rushing waters in the cold weather, we then took off to Lucerne. En route we stopped at Zurich for spicy *shawarma* at a Lebanese Kebab shop. From Zurich, it was just an hour and a half drive to Lucerne. One of the most scenic cities in Switzerland, Lucerne maintains its quaint old-world charm. The beautiful lake, with its calm waters, brings pride to the already picturesque town. The Chapel Bridge, which is a wooden footbridge across the river Reuss, is one such beautiful structure of the city. The bridge, decked with red flowers on the sides, appears like a floral path across the waters. The night stay was in the suburbs of Interlaken, a city which was an hour's drive from Lucerne.

The following morning, we spent some time at the Interlaken Monastery and Castle. The window designs of the Castle and the bell tower give a glimpse of the 14th century architectural style. We couldn't spend much time as I had a flight to catch from Geneva. It was a three hour drive and I was in time for my flight. I thanked Segar for showing me around, and after bidding each other bye, he left for Lyon and me for Rome.

The three day trip across Switzerland pushed my limits. Well, I didn't have the time and that was the best I could do with the little time and resources I had. The drive around Switzerland was an out-of-the-world experience. We drove through many tunnels and picturesque villages. The green pastures, the blue sky, the chilly climate, and vast cattle in the countryside made me think that perhaps Switzerland was a portrayal of paradise on earth. The beauty of the Swiss country was overwhelming for me. There was abundance everywhere. Everything seemed to be perfect. So perfect that at times I couldn't comprehend the fact that this was the same earth I live in too. I can't forget the moments when I wanted to be left alone at the Rhine Falls just to hear the music of the thundering waters, to stand with my back to the gusting winds at the dunes, to sit quietly and watch the placid waters in Lucerne. Though I did spend time in all these places, my heart craved for more.

The airplane was on time in Geneva. I boarded the flight and once I settled, I closed my eyes, thinking of the excitement Italy had to offer.

XV

I slowly opened my eyes and my Indian friend Deepak was deep asleep, with his head on his wife's shoulder. The crew was distributing food and I was in no mood for eating. I spotted a crew member walking down the aisle. I raised my hand to grab her attention. She came to me and I said, "Please don't serve me food now. I am going to sleep." She replied, "Sure, Sir! I will keep it ready for you once you wake up." I smiled and said, "That's very nice of you. Thank you." She smiled and left. I closed my eyes to get back to my world of reminiscence.

It was around 8 PM when I landed in Rome, Italy. After collecting my bags, I took a bus to Roma Termini, the central railway station. I booked a homestay near the station for convenience of travel. The host was an old man in his 70s and he couldn't speak English. He was able to understand Spanish as Spanish and Italian are somewhat like cousins. He gave me all the information about the city and the tourist spots, wished me a pleasant stay, and left. After a shower, I got down the building and took a walk to scan the neighbourhood. I found a shop across my building serving pizzas. It was quite a breezy day I ordered a pizza with a beer and savoured my Italian dinner at leisure on the tables laid on the pavement.

Rome is a treasure trove of ancient historical sites that showcases the illustrious Roman culture. Forget the whole of Rome, even to see the highlights, would take more than a week as it has so much to offer for a curious traveller. Due to time constraints, I had planned a two day tour of Rome. My homestay at Roma Termini was just a kilometer and a half from the Colosseum, one of the Seven Wonders of the World, and an imposing landmark in the city of Rome. Early in the morning, I started my walk on the stone-paved roads which were lined up with many restaurants on the way, serving famous Italian delicacies. In less than ten minutes, I reached the site. I was baffled at the expanse of this massive structure which is an oval-shaped amphitheatre. The 2,000 year old colossal complex served the purpose of hosting gladiatorial games, which saw nearly 400,000 people die in the fights. I bought the tickets and entered the monument. It was mostly in ruins but some restoration had taken place to give an idea of how it was in those days. Inside, there were seating arrangements for people, probably according to their social ranking, and at a rough estimate, they could seat around 50,000 spectators. I could recollect portions from the history books which I had studied and also scenes from the movie *Gladiator*, which was one of my favourites, as I walked around the Colosseum.

A five minute walk from there took me to the Palatine Hill, also known as the nucleus of the Roman Empire. Considered to be the home of the aristocrats and emperors, most of the structures were in ruins. Adjacent to the Palatine Hills was the Roman Forum, which was probably a marketplace or a social gathering place to conduct criminal trials. The Forum housed most of the old and essential buildings. Despite being in ruins, the surviving tall columns and platforms stunned me.

A three minute walk from the Roman Forum is the Trajan's market. These were probably offices which formed part of the Forum. A ten minute walk from there took me to Italy's most famous fountain, the Trevi Fountain. It is the largest fountain in the city completed by the renowned Italian architect Giuseppe Pannini in the Baroque style of architecture. There was a huge rush of tourists and it took me some time to push myself closer to the structure. The fountain is a masterpiece of art. The waters in the fountain cascade in three steps and get collected in a small square in the front. Statues of the Sea Gods and horses adorn either side with the Palazzo Poli in the background. At the fountain, I saw people throwing coins in the fountain pool. It was then that I learned about the legend that if you throw one coin, you will come back to Rome; two coins meant that you will come back and fall in love; three coins meant that, you will come back, fall in love and marry. Well, thanks to the legend, the tourists were showering coins in the fountain. It would have been a good source of income to whosoever maintained the site.

Next in line was the Spanish Steps at a distance of around three quarters of a kilometer. The Spanish steps are a set of steep steps from the Piazza di Spagna up to the Trinitàdei Monti church. Again there were hordes of tourists, and unfortunately, I didn't get a chance to sit on the steps as it was closed for restoration at that time. Walking another kilometer and a half, I reached the Pantheon, a well-preserved monument, once a Roman temple, and later a Catholic Church. It houses the tombs of the famous artist Raphael and several Italian Kings. It was already evening; I had walked enough for the day and I was too tired to take another step. I looked for the city bus service and found I couldn't buy the tickets on the bus, but only at the tobacco shops near the stop. I purchased mine and boarded the bus. Watching the city as the bus rode, scenes from the Audrey Hepburn movie, *The Roman Holiday,* started playing in my mind. As I reached Roma Termini, I walked to my pad to retire for the day.

Vatican City, a country within Rome, was next in line. I took off early in the metro from Roma Termini and within 45 minutes I got down at S. Pietro metro station. I walked for another 20 minutes, and found the tall walls of the Vatican City. The tourists crowded the entry gates; there were tour guides holding flags, keeping their flock together. I had taken a ticket for the Sistine Chapel, which is the most visited monument, a site of papal conclaves where new popes are selected and hence its importance in the Catholic World. After the regular checks, I stood in the line leading to the Chapel. The pathway leading to the Chapel had sculptures on the sides and golden paintings on the ceiling. As the line was slowly moving forward, most of the tourists, including me, were busy taking pictures with their mobile phones and cameras. When the entrance arrived, we had to switch off our cameras and maintain silence. The second I ventured inside, I was astounded. I took a vantage seat in the hall and started to scan the art. Frescoes by the Renaissance masters adorned the walls and the famous ceiling had the outstanding works of Michelangelo viz., *The Creation of Adam, The Fall and Expulsion from Garden of Eden, The Flood, The Deluge,* etc. I was neither a connoisseur of art nor a student attempting to study. I was just a layman watching the thoughts of a creative mind being transformed into art, as reflected in the frescoes and on the ceiling. It had transported me to a new colourful world where the biblical stories encircled me in different hues. I couldn't stop wondering how a man could paint the ceiling, labouring for four years, and how much thought and process would have gone into creating this masterpiece which, centuries later, I would be blessed to see. It was nothing but the sheer proof of a thinking mind at display. Here, I couldn't help but recollect the words from *The Atlas Shrugged* by Ayn Rand, where the author interprets a lighted cigarette between the fingers as "a manifest of the powerful mind, where man has tamed fire, a dangerous element of nature, and kept it at his fingertips."

From the Sistine Chapel, it was on to St. Peter's Basilica. The greatest of all churches in the Christian world, it also houses many masterpieces of Renaissance and Baroque art along with numerous statues. Legend has it that St. Peter, the chief of Jesus's apostles, was buried here. Coming out of the Basilica, there is a grand plaza called the St. Peter's Square, which is the core of the Vatican City. At the centre is a tall Egyptian Obelisk. Columns and pilasters encircle the plaza in an arcade of four rows which gave it a majestic look.

That wound my tour of Rome. Rome, one of the beautiful cities of the world, is an excellent repository of art and architecture. The study of world history is inconsequential if Rome doesn't figure in it. The city still maintains its ancient appearance, and if a Roman from the Renaissance period returns, he wouldn't feel much of a difference as the city has carried its historical legacy and heritage through the centuries. The brick-paved roads, the old drinking water taps found around Rome are a testimony to it. A tour of the city took me back to ancient days and replenished me with much information on history and art. Even today, when I close my eyes and think of Rome, the picture of the magnificent city flashes in mind with all its elegance.

The same day after having finished my tour of the Vatican, I took a train to Florence. It was an hour and a half long journey. Trains in Italy have a different system. Once you purchase the ticket, you have to go to a machine on the platform and insert it to get the ticket validated. I didn't know that, and I boarded the train and took my seat. The ticket examiner on verification said it was an offence not to get the ticket punched. As I was a foreigner, he said he would do the punching for me and advised me to be careful next time. I reached Florence the same evening and, as usual, picked up a homestay near the station. It was a Chinese household. They gave me full access to their kitchen and also to the food and fruits stored in the refrigerator.

The next morning, I took a train to Pisa. It was an hour long ride. There was a bus stop outside the train station and I bought my ticket from a tobacco shop, as is the norm in Italy, and boarded the bus. It was a 10 minute ride, and once I got off the bus, the marvel was right there across the road. It was a complex with the Pisa Cathedral, the Leaning Tower, and the Baptistery. The main attraction being the Tower, hordes of tourists were around the structure taking pictures. Due to some repair works, public entry to the Pisa was not allowed. I had to console myself with enjoying the beauty from the outside. One thing I found in common throughout Europe is that the sky was always a perfect blue. With the pitch blue sky and the lush green lawn, the milky white tower and the Cathedral were a painter's delight and so captivating. I took the next train back to Florence as I had to catch a train to Venice and had only a few hours left to explore Florence.

Getting down at Florence, I ran to the Duomo. The Piazza del Duomo is located at the centre of the city and very close to the Rail station. The Duomo is a cathedral in Florence, which got its name from the enormous octagonal dome at its east end. Said to be the birthplace of the Renaissance, the cathedral is yet another architectural marvel. I spent about 30 minutes around the place, then went back to pick my things and rush to Venice. Honestly, I do not enjoy running from place to place. Fitting the Swiss trip in the itinerary, however, made it a tight schedule. I had to ration time for Italy. I missed *David* by Michelangelo on this trip. I hope that maybe on my next trip I will visit it.

It was a two-and-a-half hour journey from Florence to Venezia Mestre. It was the last stop. I got down and checked in at a homestay, which was again a Chinese household. Venezia Mestre is in the mainland, and Venice is a conglomeration of islands separated by canals and linked by bridges. The distance between Mestre and Venice is just 10 km and takes less than 10 minutes by train. Moreover, being a significant tourist attraction, stay in Venice is highly expensive, which explains my stay at Mestre. I spent the evening walking the streets of Mestre and ended my day in a bar which was playing rock music.

After breakfast, which was complimentary at the homestay, I walked to the train station and took a train to Santa Lucia, the train stop for Venice. In ten minutes, I was in Venice and getting out of the station, a few steps down, I was at the canal. People were waiting in line to take the river cruise. I decided to walk, and that became one of my favourite walks of life. Going down the banks of the canal, I crossed over a bridge to get to the other side and continued my walk. There was no destination in my mind. It was just a walk to whichever place it took me. There were small lanes between old buildings with tall brick walls, and at times it would lead to a dead-end, and I had to take another path to find my way out. There were hundreds of bridges connecting the banks of the canal. It was a scenic view to see a gondola - a traditional flat bottom Venetian rowing boat, pass by. With a glass of wine in hand, sitting in a gondola with your darling by your side, and sailing through the canal maze, enjoying the picturesque view is what I say would be a romantic ride. Many couples were enjoying themselves on the gondola ride. Some gondoliers played romantic music too.

Crisscrossing Venice on foot, I ended up at a far off place. I visited a small roadside restaurant to relax as I had been walking for nearly two hours. It was there that I met a boy selling masks. Venice is famous for its centuries old tradition of wearing masquerade masks during carnivals. Though not a carnival time, tourists do buy masks as souvenirs. Looking at me, the boy started to speak in Hindi. He was quick to recognise that I was from India. With my broken Hindi, I began to converse. The boy said that he was from Bangladesh and that there was a substantial Bangladeshi population in Venice selling souvenirs and that most of the gondoliers were Bangladeshis too. I bought a mask from him and bought him a gelato, a famous ice-cream from Italy. He then asked me if I missed Indian food. I said it had been a long time. He asked me to follow him and took me to a small shop selling *rotis* and curry. It was such a small shop that it would never figure in any lonely planet book or site. I had a sumptuous meal and thanked the boy for showing me a good food joint in Venice. He then asked me to visit Saint Mark's Basilica and the tower which were nearby. Thanking him, I went to Saint Mark's Basilica, the most famous of the city's churches and one of the best-known examples of Italio-Byzantine architecture. It has a foyer before the entry to the main church. The mosaics of its domes and arches are drawn from and depict biblical stories. It is also a home for many treasures brought from the Crusades. The St. Mark's tower was just adjacent to the Basilica and it is the tallest structure in Venice. A climb up the tower gives a panoramic view of Venice. After I visited the Basilica and the tower, I took the river cruise and got back to Santa Lucia and from there to Mestre. The following day I took a train to Milan. I couldn't find time to go around Milan and the places I saw in the city were the train station and the airport. From Milan, it was back to India.

A fast-paced journey it was; I had the opportunity to see most of the places despite the time constraints. It was a memorable trip on many counts. I had the pleasure of traversing Venice on foot, exploring the ancient city of Rome, immerse in its history, visit the Pisa, a World Wonder, and rush through the Duomo in Florence. I realised that Italy was a breed apart from rest of the Europe. It has a unique climate, culture, and history, which differentiates it from other countries. Whether it is its Mediterranean cuisine with a unique flavour or the marvellous paintings, sculptures, or architecture, the country offers it all. Italy is a treasure house and it deserves at least a month's travel. I feel guilty for not being able to devote that much time. Well, I still have a lot more to travel in Europe and would try to revisit Italy for my love for the place and its glory and eminence.

The thought of Italian food gave me hunger pangs. I turned to look at Deepak; he was busy in a romantic conversation with his wife. I got up and walked to the pantry. The air hostess who said that she would save my food was there smiling at me. Before I could ask, she said, "Sir, I think you would like to eat something. Shall I send your food to your seat?" I said, "Yes, please!" I smiled and walked back to my seat.

XVI

My food arrived at my seat and Deepak turned to me and said, "You must be pretty tired. You didn't even have your food while they were serving!" I said, "Yes, it has been long journey and I am a bit tired." "Yes, I can understand. I was talking to you about my trip and you went off to sleep." he said. I smiled at him while devouring the chicken meal. He then asked me, "Well, where are you coming from?" I said, "The US." and avoided telling about my travel details. "Which part of the US did you go to?" he continued. I said, "Miami." to keep the conversation short. He further pursued his questioning. "You have a US visa and I guess it must be business, right? You don't seem like a person who goes backpacking and travelling!"

There was a sense of joy on his face as if he had figured out something. I just smiled, revealing nothing. He now switched to advising mode. "You should see a lot of places. Look at me! In this week's time, I have been to Spain and France. Work will always be there. We should find time to travel." I agreed with him on this idea. He then continued, "You know what? Next month I am planning to go to Penang, Malaysia with my wife." Despite the fatigue on my dished-out face, I tried to look enthusiastic and said, "Wow, that's wonderful. It's good that you love travelling! It's great!" He was happy to receive my comments. I slowly got up with my tray in hand and walked to the pantry to hand it over. When I returned, Deepak was again busy cuddling and was in a romantic chat with his wife. I sat down with my head leaning against the window. The crew dimmed the lights and most of the passengers were in deep sleep. I too closed my eyes. My thoughts, as usual, took me to another journey in Europe.

It was the end of October when I landed in Brussels. It was autumn and the city was already freezing. I took a metro from the airport to the Brussels Midi station. I was at a homestay close to the station and this time I was with a Lebanese family. They gave me a cosy room to rest and also information about the city and the food joints. It was an icy cold morning when I stepped out for my city walk tour. There was a cafeteria adjacent to the house where I had some hot chocolate and a sandwich for breakfast. It was a kilometer walk in the cold weather from the cafe to the Grand Place or *Grote Markt* as it is called. It's quite common in European cities to have a grand plaza or a square surrounded by buildings. The Grand Place in Brussels was no different. However, the lively, cobbled square with the surrounding guild houses made it more impressive. There are many famous buildings around the square - the 15th century town hall, the Maison du Roi, which presently houses the Museum of Brussels, Le Pigeon, the house where the famous author Victor Hugo lived during his exile, Le Roy d'Espagne, which was once a baker's guild and now a popular bar, the Maison des Ducs de Brabant, which had seven houses under one massive façade are a few examples to illustrate. Just off the Grand Place is the bronze statue of Everard t'Serclaes, which legend says brings good luck to those who touch its arm. As expected, there was a small crowd trying to touch the hand of the statue. Hope lady luck smiles on them!

A few minutes' walk from the Grand Place is the world-famous Manneken Pis. A symbol of the Belgians' sense of humour, it is a small bronze fountain sculpture depicting a boy urinating in the fountain pool. A minute walk from there is the famous cartoon mural on the side of a gift shop building featuring Tintin, Snowy & Captain Haddock. Walking further down the narrow streets, I passed the St. Nicholas Church, a famous landmark, and La Monnaie De Munt, Brussels' famous Opera house. A two minute walk from there took me to the Jeanneke Pis, which is a modern fountain sculpture, intended to form a counterpoint to Manneken Pis. It is a sculpture of a girl squatting and urinating. A kilometer walk down the road took me to the imposing Royal Palace of Brussels, another famous landmark in the city. I wound up my tour at that point and walked back to my homestay. Brussels is famous for chocolates and I didn't miss the opportunity to savour the famous Godiva chocolates of Belgium with great relish.

Early the next day, I was supposed to take a flight from Brussels to Berlin. Somewhere at midnight, I received a message informing me that the airline had cancelled its flight to Berlin. As it was a budget airline, no alternate arrangements were made, but for promptly refunding my money. I immediately had to book a bus to Berlin online, which was to leave at 7 AM in the morning. To be on time at the bus station, I had to wake up early. It was a cold morning. I could feel the chillness despite wearing two shirts, a sweater, a jacket, and a shawl covering my ears. The local metro took me to Brussels North station and I was on time for my bus ride to Berlin.

It was a twelve hour drive to Berlin, and as usual, I spent my time looking at the Belgian-German countryside. Our bus stopped at Dusseldorf after a three hour ride and the driver informed the passengers that the bus would halt for 30 minutes. It was enough for me to go for a short walk around the Dusseldorf bus station and get the feel of the city. I timed my watch for 15 minutes and walked through the lanes opposite the bus station, picked up a *kebab* from the Doner Kebab shop, and was right back on my bus five minutes early. The bus drove via Hanover and it was around 7 PM when I reached the Central Bus Station, Berlin. It was already dark by then and Berlin was colder than Brussels. The Kaiserdamm metro station was the closest. I took a train to Eberswalder Strasse and from there, I walked to my homestay. It was a silent locality with a tram service just at the doorstep and the Berlin war memorial a kilometer away. My host was German and provided me with ample information about the city.

Berlin, like any other European city, is replete with edifices and is always a subject of study for a student of architectonics. The *Rotes Rathaus*, or the Red Town Hall, the Berlin Cathedral, the imposing Protestant Church with a large turquoise-coloured dome, the Humboldt University complex are a few to name. The Gendarmenmarkt, a square with a statue of Friedrich Schiller adorning the centre, is also a site for buildings like the Concert hall and the French and German Churches. The architecture of these buildings showcases the artistic skills of the builders dating back to the 17th century. The famous Brandenburg Gate, built by King Frederick William II in the 18th century, served as a critical entry point to the city of Berlin. A statue of a chariot pulled by four horses, also known as the *Quadriga*, adorns the top of the Gate. The Gate, once a symbol of the German division during the Cold War, is now a national symbol of peace and unity.

Despite being ravaged by World Wars, Nazism, and Communism, the city has maintained its cultural integrity and has bounced back to prominence. Numerous monuments speak of the atrocities of the Nazi times. The Bebelplatz, a public square, is remembered for the shocking book-burning incident of 1933, where around 20,000 books opposed to Nazism, including writings of Karl Marx and Sigmund Freud, were reduced to ashes.

Checkpoint Charlie or Checkpoint C, a Berlin Wall crossing point between East Berlin and West Berlin during the Cold War, speaks of the days of Communism. This point has now become a famous tourist attraction after the fall of the Wall in 1989.

The Jewish Holocaust Memorial is a monument dedicated to the thousands of Jews who were wiped off during the Nazi regime. Designed by an American architect, it was constructed with around 2,700 rectangular stone blocks on a vast land with similar length and width but varying height. Visitors can walk between the slabs on a cobbled pathway. Unlike other memorials, this one doesn't have inscriptions of the name of the victims.

The Wall Memorial conveys an impression of how the border fortifications developed until the end of the 1980s. It has preserved the historical remnants and showcased the events till its fall. There was a tower near the site and I walked up to have a bird's-eye view of the Wall. A small portion of the Wall lives as a memory of the cruel past. The centre displayed stories of people who tried to escape but were captured. The remnants of the Wall looked like scars on a beautiful city. It was an intense experience at the memorial.

The Germans have emerged more resilient and moved out of their unfortunate past. They have disassociated themselves from anything that has a fibre of Nazism. I have this story told about Hitler's bunker by my host. He said that the Germans didn't want a monument to come by on the place where Hitler died, and so to make it mundane, they constructed a car park and a children's play area. So what they say was a Hitler's bunker is just another parking lot and a place for children to play. Now it has become another legend. These things speak about the spirit and the grit of the Germans who had seen enough in a century.

A trip to Berlin doesn't end without visiting the Reichstag. A couple of months before this trip, I had applied for a permit to visit the Reichstag, the German Parliament. I had meticulously planned my travel programme only after getting permission for Reichstag. I was very eager to see the building as I had learned a lot about it. On the scheduled day of the visit, I took a tram and was there an hour before my appointed time. Some tourists who had applied for entry were standing in the line. There was a mandatory check of documents, and after that, I joined the group assigned to me. I was welcomed by a person who was my guide for the next two hours in the Reichstag. He took us to the parliament floor and other offices in the Reichstag. One exciting thing shown by our guide was the graffiti on the walls of the Reichstag. He then narrated the history behind that. During the Battle of Berlin in 1945, the Red Army captured the Reichstag. It was considered a significant victory for the Russians for its perceived symbolic significance. On winning, the Russian soldiers scribbled on the walls of the Reichstag which the Reichstag still preserves as the Soviet graffiti to this day. My trip to the Reichstag ended with a visit to the Glass Dome. On the way up to the dome, there were photographs and news clippings posted on a circular panel depicting the modern history of Germany. On the top is a 360 degree view of the Berlin cityscape, which was indeed a breathtaking view.

While I was at Berlin Cathedral, I happened to meet a young tourist who was standing next to me and looking intensely at the monument. We both smiled at each other. He introduced himself as Ahmed from Pakistan and I introduced myself to him. He was a young student from Lahore who had come on a student exchange programme to the University of Hamburg. It being a weekend, he came down to Berlin to visit the city. While I was talking to him in English, he was conversing in Hindi or maybe Urdu. I told him that I couldn't converse in Hindi well, and he was shocked, for he was under the impression that all Indians speak Hindi fluently. I explained about the linguistic profile of India and he was all ears. We became friends instantly. Talking our way through, we visited the tourist spots together.

After we wound up our day at Brandenburg gate, I invited him to come over to my place for dinner. He was very particular about halal food because of his religion. I assured him of a Lebanese kebab joint near my homestay, which served halal food. He accepted and we took a metro to reach the place. My host had earlier mentioned one of Berlin's best flea markets which took place in the vicinity of Mauerpark on Sundays. He asked me not to miss it. The day being Sunday, Ahmed and I went right away to the market which was just a few hundred meters from my place. Apart from furniture and antiquities, the market sold almost everything under the sun. I purchased a sweatshirt and some homemade eatables which were prepared and sold by some German families. There was beer, music, and karaoke; it was like a carnival. The people, too, were in a holiday mood, enjoying it all. After spending some time at the market, I took Ahmed to the Lebanese food shop as promised. We had a sumptuous dinner and after chatting for a while, he left for his hostel. It is nice to make friends during travel who share the same frequency. After Berlin, it was Prague, Czech Republic.

Prague is one of the loveliest cities I have ever been to. It is a city full of tourist's delights and emblematic monuments. The city has the same positive vibration which I felt at the Times Square, New York. The cobbled streets of the town lead a tourist to discover its wonders. I was staying at the Brewery Hotel in the heart of the city and just ten minute walk from the iconic Charles Bridge. The hotel staff welcomed me with a glass of locally brewed Czech beer. I became an instant fan. All through the stay, I spent my evenings sipping this wonderful liquid. Stepping out, I found a busy city with people waiting at tram and bus stations. The streets were lined up with restaurants serving food at the tables laid out on the pavements. Prague had cold weather but it was much warmer than Berlin. It gave me a beautiful day to explore the fascinating city of Prague.

As is common to all European cities, Prague too has a historic square in the old town quarters surrounded by buildings boasting of Gothic architecture. The old town hall, the St. Nicholas Church, the towers of the Tyn church – all add much splendour to the colourful square. An important attraction at the square which intrigued me is the old astronomical clock of the 15th century which is still operational. Apart from telling time, it tells the date and also shows astronomical and zodiacal information. The combination of a beautiful design with the mechanical show that it provides every hour makes it unique and attracts crowds which gather below the clock to see it in action. One interesting fact to be noticed in the houses of the Old town area is that each home has a symbol chiselled or painted on the façade. They must have some link to the history of the house or the trade practised there.

Another exciting site is the Church of St. James. Once I stepped into the nave, I was stunned to see a withered severed black arm hanging on a hook on the ceiling. Legend has it that around the 16th century, a man entered the church to pray, but his eyes caught the attention of the jewels adorning Mother Mary. He climbed up to grab one when the statue broke its pose and caught hold of the thief's hand. She held him all night, and when in the morning the monks came and discovered him, they tried to let the hand go free, but it wouldn't. The icon of Mary would never let go. With no options left, they butchered the arm, and once done, the image let go of the arm and returned to its serene pose. The butchers then hung the severed arm on the ceiling as a warning. Sounds interesting, doesn't it?

The Lennon Wall was another site that attracted me. With the assassination of John Lennon, the wall had come up. It was a place to vent out political grievances against the communist regime with John Lennon-inspired graffiti and lyrics from Beatles' songs.

The Charles Bridge is a historic bridge built in the 14th century across the Vltava River in Prague connecting the Prague Castle and the old town. There are several black statues at regular intervals adorning the bridge. One of the figures is that of John of Nepomuk. Legend says that touching the falling priest on the plaque brings luck and ensures your return to Prague. I was not surprised to see tourists trying to reach the plate. The plaque has a shine due to countless people touching it over centuries. One of the most important cultural institutions of the Czech Republic is Prague Castle, which is now the office of the President of the Czech Republic. The 8th century castle was a seat of power for the kings and emperors for ages. It also treasures the Crown Jewels, the relics of Bohemian kings, precious Christian antiques, art treasures, and other historical documents.

Apart from visiting the attractions, I enjoyed my rides in the tram, where I would pick up a random tram and go to its final destination. I would then walk down a distance and pick up another tram to reach my hotel. This way, I was able to mingle and interact with the people. It was an adventure in its own way.

Prague to Vienna was a four and a half hour ride on a bus and it was past noon when I arrived at the Hilton Vienna Plaza Hotel there. Vienna is a city on the Danube River, and its residents included Mozart, Beethoven, and Sigmund Freud, which explains the artistic and intellectual legacy of the town. The city also boasts of imposing palaces and opera houses like the Belvedere Palace, Schönbrunn Palace, the Hofburg Palace, each a masterpiece of architecture of its own accord.

The Hofburg Palace is a colossal edifice and my all-time favourite. Constructed in the 13th century, it expanded over the years into a huge palace complex. It continues to be the seat of the Austrian Federal President today. The palace faces the famous Heldenplatz square, where Hitler made his announcement to annex Austria. Vienna also had its share of agony with Nazism. The monument at Albertinaplatz, which depicts a Viennese Jew forced to kneel and scrub the streets after Austria was annexed by Hitler's Germany in 1938, gives us the magnitude of public degradation and cruelty that followed the annexation.

Keeping the history of Heldenplatz aside, I fell in love with the magnificence of the place. It was my last day in Vienna and also the last day of my tour of Europe. After walking around the palace and the lawn, I found a bench facing the Hofburg palace in the garden. I sat down on the bench. On my sides, I could see avenues with colourful trees. Behind me was a big road with trams passing by periodically. I took out my Snickers bar and a banana, which I had brought with me and started to eat, pampering myself with a magnificent view. The air was fresh and the sky pitched blue. The entire situation looked to me like a piece of a brilliant artistic creation. Like they say in Hindu temples, one may not close one's eyes but pray with eyes open, enjoying the beauty of the deity; I also didn't close my eyes. Instead, I was indulging in the architectural marvel in front of me and the scenic beauty. It was a fusion of a human-made wonder and a trait of nature at play before me. I was letting all my senses absorb whatever possible from the fusion, the scenic view, the floral smell, the cool weather, and the sound of the soft breeze. The forlornness didn't unsettle me; instead, it was an inclination being isolated.

Not all incidents were good. There are some which made me feel unpleasant. As I said, I was staying at the Hilton, and there was this executive lounge where I had breakfast in the mornings and drinks and dinner in the evenings. It was a cool place as one got to meet a lot of travellers. One evening I was sitting at a corner table near the window, which could accommodate only two. I was having a drink with some snacks. Close to my table was a bigger table which could accommodate four people. A white couple with serious demeanour who didn't even respond to my welcome smile, had come to sit there. I didn't mind and was having a drink and talking to a friend over the phone. The lounge was quite noisy with people having drinks and chatting. I went to the counter to get a refill, and when I returned, the white man asked me, "Hey, could you leave and sit elsewhere?" I didn't understand and was confused. I asked him, "Sir, I don't understand. Could you tell me what you want?" He again said with his voice much sterner, "Can you go and sit elsewhere? We are not comfortable here with you and your phone calls." I felt offended when they asked me to choose another table as they were not comfortable with me. I said, "Sir, I was sitting here for past one hour and you had come just now. I think it isn't fair to ask me to leave." He raised his voice a bit. There was this American who was sitting across saw the whole scene, came to my rescue and said to the couple, "It's you who has to leave. This guy has been here for quite some time." The couple left at last with scorn on their face. The American looked at me and said with a shrug, "Racist guys! You chill, bro." and gave me a closed fist bump. My first experience with racism was indeed painful and demeaning. Thanks to the American tourist who put off an awkward situation and made me feel comfortable!

While I was deep in my thoughts, I felt a tap on my shoulder. I woke up and saw the air hostess looking at me. She said, "Sir, pull your seat up and fasten your belt. We shall be landing shortly." I was wondering how fast time flew by. I sat straight put on my jacket and looked at Deepak who was waiting to land in Delhi.

XVII

The flight touched down at New Delhi's Indira Gandhi International Airport. It was a smooth landing, and none felt a jerk or a shake. I often wonder how skillful the pilot must be to make such a perfect landing. The flight slowly reached its lot and was waiting for the aerobridge to attach. As usual, the impatience of the passengers came to the fore. They pulled their bags from the overhead bin and started crowding the aisle. Once the doors opened, everyone started to rush towards the door. Deepak, with his bags ready in his hands, looked at me, and said, "It was nice meeting you, bro! We'll catch up some time!" I smiled and said, "Sure, will do, and once again enjoy your trip to Malaysia." "Thanks, bro. And you, too, start travelling." I smiled at him and nodded my head. I walked out of the aircraft weary - it was a long walk to the immigration and from there to the baggage carousel. The Dallas IT guy spotted me there, came to me and said, "It was nice knowing you, sir! Have a pleasant flight to Chennai." "You too have a pleasant flight. It was nice knowing you too!" While I was bidding him bye, my baggage arrived, and I left the arrivals with the IT guy still waiting for his luggage to arrive.

Getting out of International Arrivals, I walked to the Domestic Departures for my flight to Chennai. After getting my boarding pass and clearing security, I walked straight to the food court to eat some breakfast. The long journey had made me ravenous. The first food stall that hit my eye was busy with people. I waited for my turn and chose a South Indian breakfast which was exorbitantly priced. I felt a bit relaxed after eating. There were still four hours to go for my flight and I started looking for a chair to relax when I saw this travel lounge just across the food court. I thanked God and walked to the lounge and flashed my travel card. I was welcomed by a pretty girl who gave me my Wi-Fi password and said, "Welcome, sir. We have a wide range of breakfast buffet for you to choose!" I immediately started cursing myself. I had just paid through my nose to get a breakfast plate at the food court and here there was a wide range of food options for free! Had I just turned my head and looked around, I would have seen the lounge. I then recollected the words of the girl at the hotel in Istanbul who said, "I think you have a habit of losing money." I walked inside, sighing heavily at the breakfast spread, and picked up a cup of coffee before taking a seat at a cosy dark corner.

The flight information monitor displayed that my flight was due for departure in three and a half hours. It had been nearly twenty four hours of travel from Miami, and time just whizzed by while I was reminiscing my journeys. When I look back at myself, I just cannot help but be in awe of the massive metamorphosis my life has seen. I imagine the little boy waiting for his father to come and take him on a tour; and here I am, in a lounge, waiting for the departure of my next flight. There was this kid on the train, scared to get down as it was raining and somebody had to push him out; and here I am, daring and raring to explore a country on my own. What an incredible transformation indeed! Each incident that occurred, each adventure I undertook, gave me immense experience, which had, in turn, contributed to this remarkable transformation.

During my days in school, I had consistently been an atheist; one might say, I never trusted in the existence of God. The purpose behind explaining the word is simply to separate me from the pseudo-atheists who deride and condemn Gods of different religions and convictions; thereby, unwittingly accepting his presence. From being an atheist to turning into a theist is a journey, and this journey was not a simple one. The philosophy of Ayn Rand affected me and never did I acknowledge anything which couldn't stand the trial of reason. The religious discussions I had with Mathi, the discourses I tuned in to, and the books I read, pulled me towards the realm of beliefs. I used to rationally interpret the various anecdotes and try to unearth the underlying philosophy leaving the story element aside. Visiting the *Vaishnava* temples helped me to know and comprehend the philosophy of *Vishishta-Advaitham,* where the Supreme Consciousness dwells in all things animate and inanimate, and that we are all part of the Supreme. My pursuit in the religious realm was never confined to visiting Vishnu temples but included temples of Lord Shiva too. Apart from Amarnath and Kailash Manasarovar, I had visited 10 of the 12 *Jyotirling* (the radiant sign of the all-powerful Shiva) temples and the five *Panchabhoota ling* (Shiva as represented in the five elements of nature) temples. These religious travels revealed many things. They gave me a tool to discover the purpose of life. They made me realise the sublime connection with the Supreme. They opened up a new avenue of thought and made me accept the reality. I was never a religious person, and even now, I do not claim to be so. My pursuits were purely spiritual.

Nature, too, had assisted in the process of my transformation and realisation. In my travels, I had the opportunity to relish the various facets of nature. Through the treacherous journeys in Tibet and the Himalayas, the ever-changing shades of the Manasarovar Lake, the thunder of the Niagara waters, the frothy waters of the Rhine Falls, the breezy breezes at the Dune of Pilat, the fantastic perspective on the Canyon, the massive light in an underground cavern, the conspicuous bioluminescence in San Juan, the nightfall in the Pacific, the pristine seashores of Brazil, the beautiful marine world at the Belizean reef, the thick timberlands of Costa Rica, the puffing volcanoes of Guatemala, nature had unleashed before me its grandeur and radiance. They showed me how insignificant, as a speck of dust I was, in the cosmic world. I began to realise how fallible and trivial I was, and that was the first step in the process of shedding the ego.

My travels to different nations fortified the idea of me being a part of the Supreme Consciousness. Back in my school days, I used to be very obstinate. I used to think and judge - this nation is correct, that nation isn't right; these people are cultureless, and those people are relentless. The journeys around the globe broke my horrendous suppositions and frightful legends my mind had created. The travels made me understand that even though, as individuals, we were diverse in culture, ways of life, convictions, and observations, somewhere inside, we as a whole, had similar feelings and sentiments. They were much the same as me in alternate skin and profoundly we were all connected. The second I contemplated it at a metaphysical plane, I could see the philosophy of *Vishishta-Advaitham* illustrated.

Every country I visited had something to offer, be it an experience, advice, or a glimpse of history which made me contemplate. Each was a valuable input, which, over a period of time, shaped my thoughts and personality and thereby made me a better person. The US experience in the tourist bus taught me how to behave in a crowd. A taxi driver in Guatemala tutored me on the importance of respecting people irrespective of their social status. The passengers at the airport in Rio showed me how one could be courteous. The Latin countries conveyed to me the art of living in the present. They also taught me to smile and wish when I come across a stranger.

It is quite common among people to think that their way of life is consistently prevalent everywhere and what is a no-no for them ought to be untouchable for the entire world. How I wish they had travelled places and realised they couldn't be further from the truth. Through this vast travel, I had figured out how to acknowledge different societies and regard them. I recognised that each culture is one of a kind in its manner and not to pass judgment on them from my shoes. These journeys trained me to welcome the other individual's perspective, even if it stands in opposition to mine. Each travel felt like I was being carved from the crude stone that I was to a meaningful sculpture. From a contemplative person to a social butterfly, from self-importance to regarding others' perspectives, there has been a notable change in my character. Had I not taken up travel as a passion, I would have been an awful, ghastly individual who had ill-conceived and would have kicked the bucket with no impression on this delightful world.

My thoughts gradually brought me back to the lounge; I checked my watch and the flights information monitor. The boarding was due to start in another 30 minutes. It was time for me to make a move to the departure gate. I picked my baggage and looked up the television screen which was telecasting international news. Vladimir Putin was making a speech on their country's Naval Day. There was a parade and he was accepting the honours. Suddenly the weariness of my body was overtaken by the alertness of my mind. I could sense a twinkle in my eyes and felt quite energetic. I looked at the television screen. My soul spoke out, "Hello, Russia! Here I come."

Lightning Source UK Ltd.
Milton Keynes UK
UKHW040824080321
379980UK00003B/1086

9 789354 271298